PURNELL'S Concise
Encyclopedia
IN COLOUR

ISBN 0 361 05320 7

Copyright © 1983 Purnell Publishers Limited
Published 1983 by Purnell Books, Paulton, Bristol BS18 5LQ
Made and printed in Great Britain by Purnell & Sons (Book
Production) Limited, Paulton, Bristol

PURNELL'S Concise
Encyclopedia
IN COLOUR

Adapted from Purnell's Concise Encyclopedia by
Theodore Rowland-Entwistle

Purnell

Contents

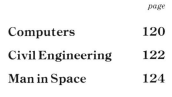

The Restless Sun

The Sun is a star. It is the star round which the Earth and other planets revolve. Compared with the millions of other stars we know about, the Sun is only of average size and brightness. But because it is much nearer than any other star it appears larger and brighter.

The Sun is a mass of hot gases, more than a million times as large as the Earth and over 300,000 times as heavy. It is about 150 million km (93 million miles) away. Light from it takes about 8½ minutes to reach Earth. It rotates on its axis about once every month.

Without the Sun, life as we know it would be impossible. It is practically our only source of light and heat. The Sun's heat and light is produced, as in any other star, when hydrogen atoms inside it join together to form atoms of helium.

The temperature at the Sun's centre has been estimated to be about 15 million degrees Centigrade. At its surface, the temperature is about 5,500°C.

Sunspots

From time to time dark patches appear on the Sun, usually in pairs or in large clusters. These patches are called *sunspots.* They are areas where the Sun's surface is slightly cooler than normal. Most sunspots last for about 20 days before disappearing. Sunspots are probably caused by magnetic disturbances deep inside the Sun.

Every 11 years or so, sunspots are very common, and there may be many groups visible at the same time. Following a peak year, sunspots appear less and less frequently, until the Sun may be completely free of them for several days at a time. Then their number increases towards the next peak year.

Particles of atoms shot out of sunspots may approach the Earth, and can cause radio interference.

Sometimes the Moon in its path round the Earth passes between the Sun and the Earth. Its shadow falls on the Earth, blotting out the Sun's light. This is a *solar eclipse.* If the Sun is completely hidden, the eclipse is *total.* When only part is hidden, it is *partial.*

Above: Cross-section of a sunspot, showing its umbra (dark central region) and penumbra (lighter outer region).

Below: The Sun's disc (*photosphere*) is surrounded by the *chromosphere,* from which great flares (*solar prominences*) leap out. Beyond is a pearly-white halo, the *corona.*

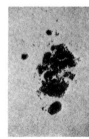

Above: A photograph of sunspots on the disc of the Sun. Sunspots usually occur in pairs or clusters. They generally last for about 20 days before disappearing.

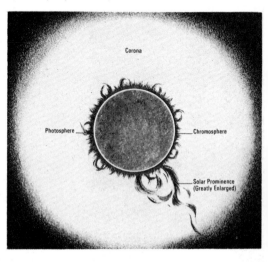

The Solar System

The Solar System in which we live consists of the Sun, the planets and their satellites (moons), and thousands of other smaller heavenly bodies, such as asteroids, comets, and meteors. The Sun is the centre of the Solar System. It holds together, by its force of gravity, all the bodies that revolve around it.

Only the Sun has any light of its own. The planets and moons shine by reflecting this light. The radius of the Solar System is more than 5,630 million km (3,500 million miles), representing the distance from the Sun to the furthest known satellite member

Comets orbit the Sun in long, oval paths. As a comet approaches the Sun it glows brightly and develops a luminous tail.

of the system, the planet Pluto. The nine planets, in order of their distance from the Sun, are Mercury (the smallest), Venus, Earth, Mars, Jupiter (the largest), Saturn, Uranus, Neptune, and Pluto.

The asteroids, or minor planets, circle the Sun just like the larger planets, but are nearly all grouped together between the orbits of Mars and Jupiter. They may be the remains of a tenth planet which has broken up.

The comets also circle the Sun, but their orbits are very *elliptical* (oval), so that their distances from the Sun vary much more than those of the planets do. Some comets pass between the Sun and the Earth and then travel right out past Pluto.

It is unlikely that ours is the only such system in the Universe. There are probably many other stars with systems of planets.

Below: The planets and their moons drawn to scale in order from the Sun: Mercury, Venus, Earth, Mars, Jupiter, Saturn, Uranus, Neptune, Pluto (distances between them are not to scale). Pluto sometimes crosses Neptune's orbit and is shown beneath that planet.

THE PLANETS

Planet	Distance from Sun (million km)	Diameter (km)	Day	Year	Satellites
Mercury	57·9	5,000	59 days	88 days	None
Venus	108·23	12,180	243 days	224·75 days	None
Earth	149·59	12,756	23 hr. 56 min.	365·25 days	1
Mars	227·72	6,760	24 hr. 37 min.	687·0 days	2
Jupiter	778·12	142,700	9 hr. 50 min.	11·86 yr.	15
Saturn	1,428·3	120,900	10 hr. 14 min.	29·46 yr.	17
Uranus	2,872·7	46,700	10 hr. 49 min.	84·01 yr.	5
Neptune	4,498·1	49,500	14 hr.	164·79 yr.	2
Pluto	5,914·3	6,400	6 days 9 hr.	248·43 yr.	None

There have been many theories attempting to explain the origin of the planets. One theory suggests that early in its life the Sun was surrounded by gases and solid particles. As these revolved with the Sun, separate masses of matter developed. These drew more particles to them, forming solid cores which slowly grew into the planets. There are other theories which suggest a sudden beginning rather than a gradual process. One such theory supposes that the Sun was once one of a pair of stars. Its partner exploded, throwing out matter, some of which was captured by the Sun's gravitational field and eventually formed the planets. The force of the explosion would have shot the remains of the other star into outer space.

Below: Mars has polar ice-caps which grow during the winter and shrink during the summer. As the ice-caps melt, part of the surface changes to a greenish colour.

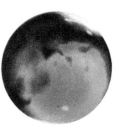

Above: Meteors are fragments, usually smaller than grapes, which circle the Sun. Sometimes they plunge into the Earth's atmosphere. Then friction makes them glow white-hot.

The Family of the Sun

Mercury is the smallest planet in the Solar System and the one closest to the Sun. It has the shortest 'year', taking only 88 Earth-days to orbit the Sun. It has a dust-covered surface.

Temperatures on this airless planet vary tremendously. During the long day it is so hot that lead would melt. At night it is far colder than anything experienced on Earth.

Venus is often visible as a brilliant white 'star', just after sunset or before sunrise. Its surface temperature is about 480°C, and it has a thick atmosphere of carbon dioxide gas. This atmosphere is clear, but exerts 100 times as much pressure as Earth's.

Moon The Moon is our nearest neighbour in space, some 384,000 km (239,000 miles) away on average. It is bleak and has no air or water. Its surface is covered with hard, loose dust and pitted with craters. It has great, dry plains and towering, jagged mountains.

Mars is the only planet having conditions even remotely similar to those on Earth. Its atmosphere contains nitrogen and carbon dioxide, but little oxygen. Its surface is scarred by the work of massive floods, but water on Mars is now only vapour or ice, never liquid. Mars' temperatures vary greatly. At noon on Mars' equator, the temperature may reach 25°C (77°F). At night it falls to about minus 40°C (minus 40°F). Tests by landing craft have found no signs of life.

Asteroids are lumps of rock and metal whose paths round the Sun lie mainly between Mars and Jupiter. Over 2,000 have now been found.

Jupiter is the biggest of the planets. It is composed, like the Sun, of hydrogen and helium. Storms rage in its atmosphere. One, known as the Great Red Spot, can be seen by telescope from Earth. It is surrounded by a ring of debris, and 14 moons.

Saturn is the second-biggest planet. It is surrounded by a huge and complex system of rings, and is orbited by 17 moons — several of them discovered by a space probe only in 1980. Its atmosphere is a mixture of hydrogen and helium.

Uranus was discovered in 1781. Through the telescope it looks like a pale greenish disc marked with faint bands. Like the other outer planets Uranus is intensely cold and has an atmosphere of poisonous gases.

Neptune was discovered in 1846 after irregularities in the orbit of Uranus led astronomers to suspect the presence of another planet comparatively nearby.

Pluto is the outermost known planet in our Solar System. Through the most powerful telescopes, it appears as little more than a yellowish spot. It was discovered in 1930.

Comets are collections of gas and dust which travel round the Sun in long, oval paths. A comet is normally invisible, but when it approaches the Sun it appears in the night sky as a bright ball with a long glowing tail.

Meteors On its journey round the Sun, the Earth collides with millions of small fragments in space. As the fragments plunge through the Earth's atmosphere, friction makes them white-hot. The result is a *shooting star*, or *meteor,* a bright line of light that flashes for a moment across the sky. Most meteors burn up, but a few are large enough to reach the ground. These are called *meteorites.*

The Earth in Space

The Seasons

Like the other eight planets in the Solar System, the Earth circles the Sun, and it takes one year to complete this journey. At the same time, it is spinning on its own axis, completing one revolution about every 24 hours. If the axis were at right-angles to the plane of the Earth's orbit round the Sun, each part of the world would have 12 hours of daylight and 12 hours of darkness the whole year round. But the Earth is like a great tilted top spinning through space. It is this 'tilt' which produces the seasons.

At one point in the Earth's orbit the North Pole leans towards the Sun and northern lands have their summer. At the same time, the South Pole leans

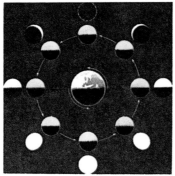

Above: Seasons are caused by the tilt of the Earth's axis as it circles the Sun. Northern and southern lands have their seasons at opposite times of the year.

Right: The phases of the Moon. We see only that part of the Moon which is illuminated by the Sun. When the Moon is between the Earth and the Sun, virtually none of it can be seen (new Moon). When the Moon is at the other side of the Earth, the whole of the illuminated side can be seen (full Moon).

away from the Sun and southern lands have their winter. Six months later, the North Pole leans away from the Sun while the South Pole leans towards it.

Time

Early man realized that time can be measured in three natural units: the *solar day*, the *lunar month*, and the *solar year*.

A solar day is the time taken for a point on the Earth's spinning surface to revolve and come back to its original position facing the Sun.

Right: Owing to the spin of the Earth, various parts of the world experience day and night at different times. When it is midday at one point on the Earth, it is midnight at the opposite side of the Earth.

A lunar month is the time between full moons and is equal to 29½ days. It is not used in modern calendars because it does not divide equally into the solar year. This is the time taken for the Earth to orbit the Sun and is almost 365¼ days.

The Romans invented the calendar that we use today. This Julian calendar (named after Julius Caesar) worked well for over 1,500 years. But the calendar year was slightly longer than the solar year, and by 1580 it was 10 days out. In 1582, Pope Gregory XIII decreed that 10 days be removed from the calendar, and made a small change in it: every 100 years, February would not have an extra day, except for the years 1600, 2000, 2400, etc. We use this *Gregorian calendar* today.

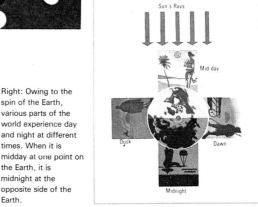

The Birth of The Earth

The Birth of the Earth

The Earth is one of a family of planets circling the Sun. Scientists believe that the planets were formed from a great cloud of gases in space. After these gases condensed to form the Earth and its surface rocks, the accumulation of radio-active materials in these rocks released heat. This melted them locally to produce pockets of molten rock, or *magma*, which are still present in the Earth's crust.

While this was happening, an immense amount of water vapour and gases was being released from the hot interior to form the primeval atmosphere, and for many millions of years our planet was masked by a dense pall of cloud. But no water appeared on the surface of the Earth, for raindrops were simply boiled back to vapour long before they could reach the intensely hot ground. At last the crustal rocks cooled sufficiently to allow rain to fall.

The Structure of the Earth

The Earth is, roughly speaking, a ball. It is rocky on the outside and is about

Below: An impression of the birth and evolution of the Earth covering a span of at least 4,500 million years.

At some point during its early life, the Earth probably passed through a semi-molten phase. This was when the heaviest minerals sank towards the centre while the lightest rose to the surface.

5½ times as heavy as a quantity of water the same size would be. Parts of its surface are very rugged, and almost three-quarters of the total surface area is covered by water.

Although scientists can learn a great deal about the Earth's *crust* by studying the rocks at the surface, they can learn about the deep interior only by studying earthquake waves. When there is an earthquake, a shock may travel a long way through the Earth, and the scientists can tell from the type of shock wave and the speed at which it travels, what type of substance it is travelling through.

The Earth's crust is divided into two main rock layers: an outer layer of *sial*, mainly silicon and aluminium, and an inner layer of *sima*, silicon and magnesium. Sial occurs as great 'rafts' floating in the heavier sima. Each of

Above: Earthquake waves have helped to prove the existence of a central core of very dense material in the Earth. For every earthquake there is a 'shadow zone' round the Earth where quake waves are not received. Those waves which miss the core travel on as normal, while those which strike it are bent inwards so they travel through it.

Right: The evidence of earthquake waves suggests that the crustal rocks, rarely more than 40 km (25 miles) thick, overlie a mantle of very dense rocks extending to a depth of 2,900 km (1,800 miles). Below this lies the Earth's core composed mainly of iron with some nickel and chromium.

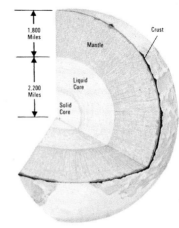

the 'rafts' is a continent.

Beneath the crust there is a layer, called the *mantle*, of very heavy rocks. The mantle surrounds the *core*, which is in two parts. The outer core is probably made from molten iron and nickel. The inner core is also believed to be composed of iron, nickel and chromium, but is solid.

Right: Much can be learned about the history of the Earth from a study of the crustal rocks. In forming the Grand Canyon, the Colorado River has cut through rock strata accumulated over 1,000 million years.

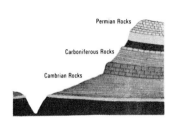

Permian Rocks

Carboniferous Rocks

Cambrian Rocks

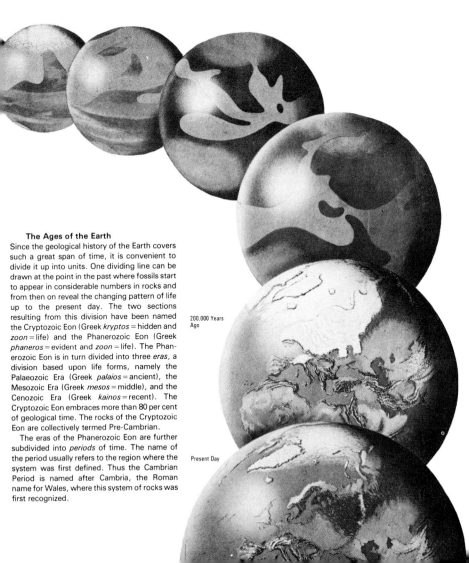

200,000 Years Ago

Present Day

The Ages of the Earth

Since the geological history of the Earth covers such a great span of time, it is convenient to divide it up into units. One dividing line can be drawn at the point in the past where fossils start to appear in considerable numbers in rocks and from then on reveal the changing pattern of life up to the present day. The two sections resulting from this division have been named the Cryptozoic Eon (Greek *kryptos* = hidden and *zoon* = life) and the Phanerozoic Eon (Greek *phaneros* = evident and *zoon* = life). The Phanerozoic Eon is in turn divided into three *eras*, a division based upon life forms, namely the Palaeozoic Era (Greek *palaios* = ancient), the Mesozoic Era (Greek *mesos* = middle), and the Cenozoic Era (Greek *kainos* = recent). The Cryptozoic Eon embraces more than 80 per cent of geological time. The rocks of the Cryptozoic Eon are collectively termed Pre-Cambrian.

The eras of the Phanerozoic Eon are further subdivided into *periods* of time. The name of the period usually refers to the region where the system was first defined. Thus the Cambrian Period is named after Cambria, the Roman name for Wales, where this system of rocks was first recognized.

Rocks and Minerals

Rocks form the material which makes up the Earth's crust. Rock consists of substances which have a definite chemical make-up, or composition. These substances are called *minerals*. Some rocks, such as chalk, contain only one mineral. Other rocks, such as granite, contain two or more minerals.

Above: Conglomerates are sedimentary rocks composed of rounded pebbles cemented by silica or lime.

Rocks

The gradual, but never-ending action of the weather breaks down even the hardest rocks into tiny particles. Streams carry the particles away and deposit them elsewhere. Over millions of years, layer upon layer of these particles builds up and gradually becomes cemented together, into a hard mass of rock.

The rock formed in this way is called *sedimentary* rock, because it is made up of layers of deposits, or *sediments*. The layers of rock are called *strata*.

Sedimentary rocks of this kind include sandstone, made up of compressed sand or quartz grains, and shale, made up of compressed clay. Large pebbles and boulders cemented together are called *conglomerate*.

Below: An unconformity in rock strata. The lower, older rocks were folded and eroded for a long time before the upper ones were laid down upon them. The irregular junction represents the passage of many millions of years.

Another kind of sedimentary rock is formed when minerals in the older rocks are gradually dissolved by water flowing over them. A stage is reached when the water evaporates and can hold no more minerals. Then the minerals in solution begin to be deposited as crystals. They gradually form layers and become rock-like. Rock salt and some limestones are of this kind. Other kinds of limestone consist mainly of the chalky remains of tiny sea creatures.

Rock strata are more or less horizontal when they are first formed at the bottom of a river or sea. In some of the limestone cliffs you see today, the strata show definite slopes, or *dips*. Some strata are even vertical. Many are bent into gentle curves, which are generally called *rock folds*. These changes were caused by movements in the Earth's crust.

Left: Stalactites and stalagmites develop where water drips out from limestone rocks. The water contains dissolved limestone. This is left behind when the water evaporates. Impurities such as iron or manganese may stain the rocks in striking colours.

Below: The Giants' Causeway on the coast of Northern Ireland is part of an old lava flow. When it cooled and contracted, it developed into six-sided columns of basalt.

Jasper

Quartz Crystals

Citrine

Amethyst

Blue Quartz

Smoky Quartz

Some of the beautiful
varieties of quartz. The
colours are due to
various impurities.

Agate

The two other kinds of rock are *igneous* rock and *metamorphic* rock. They do not have the same noticeable layers as sedimentary rocks. Igneous rocks are formed when molten material from inside the Earth cools at or near the surface. Metamorphic rocks are formed when igneous or sedimentary rocks are remelted or, owing to heat and pressure, recrystallized.

Minerals

Rocks themselves are made up of collections of substances called *minerals*. Minerals, like everything else on Earth, are composed of certain basic chemical units, or *elements*. The common mineral quartz is made up of a certain amount of the element silicon and a certain amount of oxygen.

Above: Devil's Tower, Wyoming, U.S.A., is a volcanic rock tower almost 90 metres (300 feet) tall.

Below: Diamonds are crystallized pure carbon, and are the hardest substance known.

Quartz always contains the same relative amounts of these elements.

Some minerals, such as gold, consist of only one element. They are often called *native* elements. But most minerals consist of two or more elements. Often a *metallic* element, such as iron, is combined with a *non-metallic* element, such as oxygen or sulphur. Minerals that are compounds of metal and oxygen are common, and are called *oxides*. Minerals containing metals combined with sulphur are called *sulphides*. Iron oxides and sulphides are found worldwide.

A great many minerals can be found as beautiful crystals of a variety of shapes and sizes. The hardest and rarest are used in jewellery. They are known as precious stones, or *gems*.

15

Weather and Climate

The atmosphere is a transparent envelope of gas, which we call air, hundreds of miles thick, surrounding the Earth and held to it by the force of gravity (the Earth's attraction). It is really a collection of gases, with nitrogen making up about 78 per cent and oxygen about 21 per cent. Minute quantities of a number of other gases, particularly argon, carbon dioxide, hydrogen, neon and helium, account for the remaining 1 per cent.

Without the atmosphere, life just would not exist. Not only would there be a complete absence of oxygen, the gas vital to life, but the direct rays of the Sun would sear the Earth during the day, while at night temperatures would fall far below freezing point. The atmosphere acts as a shield during the day to protect the Earth from most of the Sun's rays and as a blanket at night to hold the heat in.

Below: The world wind belts caused by heated air rising at the equator and cooler air moving in to take its place. The hot air moves towards the poles but sinks to the ground at about latitude 30°, only to rise again over colder air which is spreading out from the polar regions at about latitude 60°.

The Weight of Air
Because the air does not appear to press down on us, it seems impossible that it would weigh anything. But it certainly does. The total weight of the atmosphere reaches the staggering figure of 6,000,000,000,000,000 tonnes. The air pressure is greatest at ground level, because of the weight of the air above it. It becomes less the higher you go. At a height of nearly 50 km (30 miles) it is only one-thousandth the pressure at sea-level.

Atmospheric Layers
The atmosphere can be divided into

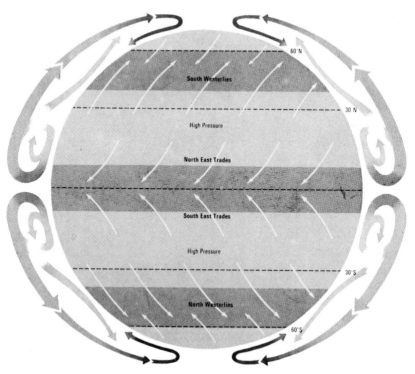

three main 'layers': the troposphere, the stratosphere and the ionosphere. The troposphere, the lowest layer, is the region of weather.

Above the troposphere lies the second layer of the atmosphere—the stratosphere. Icy winds sweep its lowest levels but the air above is perfectly calm and 'weather' ceases to exist.

Above the stratosphere lies the ionosphere, the rarefied outer layer of the Earth's atmosphere. The ionosphere is important in radio communications. It reflects long and medium radio waves back to the ground. In this way, radio messages can be transmitted round the curve of the Earth.

Weather in the Making

Different parts of the world receive different amounts of heat from the Sun. The amount of heat received from the Sun depends upon latitude, and temperatures decrease away from the equator. In high latitudes, a similar amount of the Sun's rays is spread over a greater surface area than in low latitudes (owing to the curve of the Earth), and have to travel through a greater thickness of atmosphere before reaching the ground.

This unequal heating of the Earth's surface causes movements of air—the winds. Warm air at the equator moves towards the poles, and cold air at the poles moves towards the equator. In addition, the Earth's rotation deflects the winds (to the right in the northern hemisphere, to the left in the southern hemisphere). This regular wind pattern is complicated as the Earth's surface is made up of land and water. Land heats up more quickly than water, but loses heat more quickly. This sets up pressure differences in the air over various parts of the world. The Earth's motion round the Sun, causing the seasons, further complicates matters, as do great mountain chains.

Right: Rain is caused by the rising and cooling of moist air. Convectional rain results when heated air, rising of its own accord, expands and cools.

Right: Orographic or relief rain is caused by air being forced to rise to colder levels by high land lying in its path.

Right: Cyclonic rain is caused by a mass of warm air riding up over a 'mountain' of cold air or being lifted by a 'wedge' of cold air.

Nitrogen 78%

Oxygen 21%

Other Gases 1%

Above: The composition of air.

Right: Temperatures in the atmosphere. The rise in temperature at a height of about 25–55 km (16–35 miles) is caused by a layer of ozone which absorbs ultra-violet radiation emitted by the Sun.

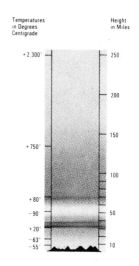

Temperatures in Degrees Centigrade	Height in Miles
	— 250
+ 2.300° —	
	— 200
	— 150
+ 750°	
	— 100
+ 80°	— 50
− 90°	
+ 20°	
− 63°	
− 55°	— 10

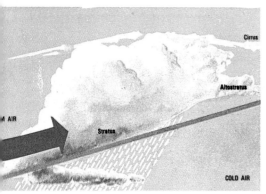

A warm front. Warm air, overtaking cooler air, rises gradually over it.

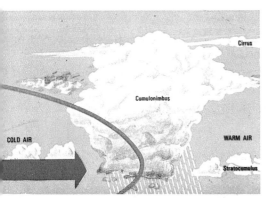

A cold front. Cold air, overtaking warmer air, burrows underneath.

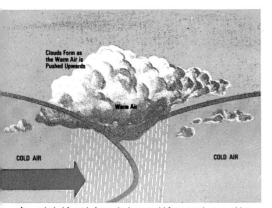

An occluded front is formed when a cold front catches up with a warm front.

As a result of all these influences, masses of air 'wander' about the Earth's surface. It is these wandering air masses that are responsible for changes in weather: they meet up with each other, they rise and fall, they are warmed and cooled, and, most important of all, they carry rain. Climate is the average kind of weather found in any particular part of the world.

Clouds and Rain

By a process called *evaporation*, water on the Earth's surface turns into a gas—water vapour—and is held in the air. The amount of water vapour a body of air can hold depends upon its temperature. The warmer the air the more moisture it can hold in the form of vapour.

When a body of air is cooled, there comes a point, known as the *dew point*, below which it is unable to hold all of its moisture in the form of vapour. The excess water vapour then *condenses* on the small particles of dust and pollen found floating in the air to form water droplets, or, if the dew point temperature is low enough, ice crystals. Condensation in the atmosphere produces cloud, or, at low levels, fog.

But the cloud particles are a long way from being raindrops, which are about a million times larger. The cloud particles get bigger as they collide with each other or as more moisture condenses on them. Then, when they reach a certain size, they tend to fall towards the ground under their own weight.

Thunderstorms

All thunderstorms form in similar conditions—where large pockets of moist air rise through cooler air. The thunder and lightning produced in a thunderstorm are caused by electrical discharges between clouds or between a cloud and the ground. Thunderstorms are rare in polar regions, and most common in the tropics. World-wide, there are more than a thousand storms going on at any one time.

The Face of the Land

The surface of the Earth is constantly being worn away by natural forces such as running water, waves, ice, and the wind. This process is called *erosion*. It takes place slowly, but surely. Even the hardest of rocks are gradually reduced to pebbles and sand. Over the past millions of years, many mountain ranges have been created and then slowly worn away.

Water Erosion

In most regions, running water has the greatest erosive effect on a landscape. Water moving along a stream bed continually picks up and deposits rock fragments. The scraping action of these fragments deepens and enlarges the stream. The faster the flow, the greater is the action. A stream in flood can easily move massive boulders a great distance. Throughout the course of a river, particles are being worn away, transported, and deposited. The finer particles are deposited as *silt* in the lower reaches of the river.

Above: A canyon on the Rio Grande. The high, vertical rock walls show the erosive power of a river.

Left: Sand deserts are produced by wind erosion in arid climates. Rock particles are reduced to sand and dust as they are dashed against solid rocks by the wind.

Below: The material eroded by the waves from one stretch of the coast is deposited later along another stretch.

On the coast, waves carrying sand and pebbles pound ceaselessly against the shore, cutting into and weakening the rock. Cliffs result from the under-cutting action of the waves which carve a notch back into the base of the rock until the material above collapses, exposing a steep bare rock face.

Ice Erosion

Glaciers, moving rivers of ice, play an important role in the sculpturing of the land. *Striated* (scratched) rocks, U-shaped valleys with truncated spurs, gouged rock basins and fiords—the un-mistakable signs of glacier erosion—are found in many parts of the world.

In the past there have been times when large areas of the land were covered by sheets of ice. These periods are known as the Ice Ages. During the most recent Ice Age, which began nearly a million years ago, much of Europe, Asia and North America lay beneath ice. As the ice advanced, it and the rocks it carried scraped the land clear of soil, levelling the surface and smoothing the mountain peaks.

Wind Erosion

In dry regions, the wind picks up particles of dust and sand and hurls them against the rock. This natural 'sand-blasting' gradually breaks down the rock into sand. Wind erosion can turn rocks into fantastic shapes.

Deposition

The debris removed by erosion is deposited elsewhere sooner or later. Most of the material transported by rivers is dropped nearer the sea, where they wind lazily in great loops, called *meanders*, across plains.

Below: In the final stages of river erosion, a river winds lazily in great loops (*meanders*) across a nearly flat plain. The sluggish water has little erosive power and instead tends to drop along its banks and on its bed the rock debris it has carried downstream.

Sometimes a large amount of material is dumped by a river where it enters the sea and its flow is checked. This material builds up to form a *delta* through which the river filters to the sea. The rest of the rock debris is dumped in the sea where it is slowly cemented into solid rock again. Earth movements may later raise these new rocks above the sea to form land.

The debris scraped from the land by glaciers is deposited as they melt. Large areas of North America and Europe are 'plastered' with boulder clay stripped from lands farther north.

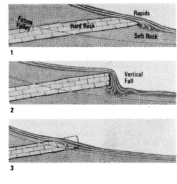

Left: An outcrop of hard rock in a river valley can cause rapids as the river wears away the softer rock (1). The undercutting action of the water may turn the rapids into a waterfall (2). The waterfall recedes as the water undercuts the hard rock (3).

Below: The Appalachians are the stumps of high mountains which have been worn away.

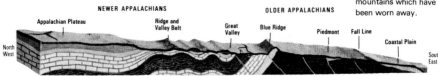

The Restless Earth

The crust of the Earth is a wrinkled 'skin', rarely more than 32 km (20 miles) thick. This crust is always in movement, producing earthquakes and volcanoes and—over very many millions of years—building mountains.

Earth movements produce three kinds of mountains: fold, block, and volcanic. *Fold mountains* form when two land masses move towards each other and compress the land at the point where they meet. The Alps are an example of fairly young folds, formed perhaps only 15,000,000 years ago when Italy came into collision with the rest of Europe.

Some movements in the Earth's

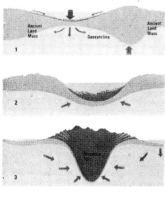

Left: Fold mountains are born under the sea as sediments collect in a slowly subsiding trough, called a geosyncline, between two adjacent land masses (1).
As the geosyncline fills the land masses on either side move towards each other (2). The mass of rock in the geosyncline is folded and buckled. The main uplift of the new mountain range comes at a later stage as the mass of rock rises slowly from the dense sub-crustal rocks to float like an iceberg in water (3).

Left: Despite the height and grandeur of mountain ranges such as the Alps, they are merely temporary wrinkles in the Earth's crust which will be eventually smoothed away by erosion. Many great ranges have been created and destroyed during the Earth's long history.

crust produce lines of weakness called *faults*. Block-like masses of the crust move along the fault lines. These blocks may rise above the general level of the land to form *block mountains*, such as the Sierra Nevada in the United States.

Volcanic mountains have a more complicated origin. Two hundred million years ago all the continents of the world were joined together in one huge land mass, which geologists call Pangaea. This super-continent broke up, and the various parts drifted slowly apart until they lie where you see them today. The surface of the Earth is covered by seven large plates, on which the continents lie, and several smaller ones. These plates are constantly moving, taking the continents with them. At some points—such as the west coast of America—one plate slips under another. At others—such as the middle of the Atlantic Ocean—new material is coming out of the interior of the Earth, so the plates 'grow'. As a result, the Atlantic is becoming about 4 cm wider every year.

Earthquakes occur along the lines where plates meet. They are caused when one plate suddenly slips against another. Most volcanoes occur along the lines where plates meet, because the Earth's crust is weakest at these points.

Volcanoes

There are many types of volcanic activity, but the term *volcano* is usually used for those cone-shaped mountains that periodically shoot out hot ashes and release lava.

Lava is molten rock (*magma*) which lies in pockets in the solid rock beneath the Earth's surface whilst the volcano is dormant.

Almost all active volcanoes are found in places undergoing earth movements. It is possible that friction between the moving rock masses heats and melts the rock, forcing it upwards

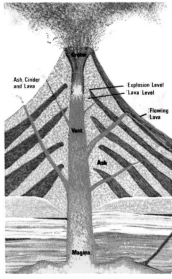

Above: A section through a volcano showing alternating beds of lava and ashes. Many volcanoes, including Vesuvius, are of this type. The ash layers are produced at the start of a new eruption.

Below: A volcanic eruption on Surtsey, an island off the coast of Iceland. The whole island is the top of a volcano, which formed in the 1960s.

through fissures and lines of weakness in the Earth's crust.

The explosive force of an eruption is mainly caused by the violent expansion of gases and water released from magma nearing the surface. The initial explosion may form a crater of considerable size. Broken rocks and cinders usually fall around the mouth, forming the cone.

If the lava contains large quantities of iron and magnesium, it is 'mobile' and flows freely, forming cones with shallow slopes called *shield volcanoes*.

Between eruptions, a volcano is said to be *dormant*.

Below: The distribution of the main earthquake regions corresponds closely with that of volcanic regions. Both are associated with the places where the great plates on the Earth's surface meet.

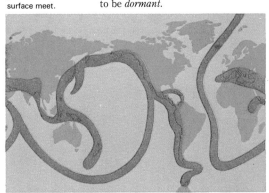

Europe

Europe is the smallest of the continents with the exception of Australia, but it is second only to Asia in population. One person in five lives in Europe. It is known as the birthplace of western civilization. Its art, political ideas, and scientific discoveries have spread all over the world. Among the 34 countries that make up Europe are the world's largest (Soviet Union), and the smallest (Vatican City).

The continent of Europe forms the western peninsula of the great Europe/Asia land mass. Its eastern limits are the Ural Mountains, and its southeastern boundary is the frontier between the Soviet Union and Turkey

Above: A cluster of houses surrounding a church is typical of many European villages.

Right: The Parthenon, a relic of the glory of Ancient Greece.

Left: Tending sheep in southern Greece, a way of life that has remained unchanged for centuries.

Right: Offering excellent opportunities to climbers and skiers, the Alps have become a major playground of Europe.

Above: Much about Europe is picturesque, although the continent is one of the most highly industrialized parts of the world.

Left: The Eiffel Tower, Paris, one of Europe's most famous landmarks.

and Iran. A small part of Turkey, north-west of the Sea of Marmara, is in Europe. The continent has an area of 10,523,000 km² (4,063,000 square miles), and a population of 676 million.

The Land

There are four main land regions. *The Alpine Mountain System* runs across southern Europe and includes the Caucasus, the Balkans, the Carpathians, the Apennines, the Alps, the Pyrenees, and the Sierra Nevada. The highest peak is Mt Elbrus (5,633 metres; 18,481 feet) in the Caucasus. *The Central Uplands* are densely forested, but they also contain some of Europe's most productive coalfields. The uplands run from Czechoslovakia, through southern Germany, central France, central Spain, and Portugal. *The Central Plains* rarely rise more than 150 metres (500 feet) above sea level. They extend from the foothills of the Ural Mountains in Russia, through Poland, northern Germany, The

Above: Austrian traditional costume. The people of Europe like to keep up their local customs in their leisure hours.

Below: Part of the Ruhr, the industrial heartland of Europe and one of the greatest concentrations of heavy industry in the world. The steel industry is based on extremely rich coal deposits.

Netherlands, Belgium, northern France, and south-eastern England. Farming is the chief occupation of this broad, fertile area. *The North-West Highlands* are craggy and steep. The highlands extend from northern Finland, through Sweden, Norway, northern and western Britain, Ireland, and western France.

Europe is well served with rivers. Most of the main ones are used as major transport routes. The longest river in Europe is the Volga which flows through the Soviet Union for 3,690 km (2,290 miles) to the Caspian Sea.

Most of Europe has a mild climate. In winter, large areas of the continent are warmed by westerly winds blowing off the Atlantic Ocean. Warm ocean currents keep most of Norway's coasts ice-free all the year round, although a third of the country lies within the Arctic Circle. In the summer, the same westerlies keep the continent cool.

Farther south, the Mediterranean

Farming and Industry

Most European farms are small but well run, and agriculture employs more workers than any other industry. Western European farmers use advanced methods and produce a very high yield of crops. Important crops include wheat, barley, oats, sugar beet, beans, peas, and tobacco.

Dairy farming is an important part of European agriculture. Denmark, Britain, and The Netherlands specialize in the production of butter, cheese, and milk. Half the exports of Denmark, Greece, Spain and Ireland consist of foodstuffs.

Europe possesses enormous centres of mining and manufacturing. The greatest of these is the Ruhr Valley, in West Germany, where vast amounts of coke, chemicals, heavy machinery, and iron and steel are produced.

A third of the world's coal is mined in Europe. The richest coalfields lie in the Soviet Union, Poland, Britain, and West Germany. The leading iron ore producers are the Soviet Union, Sweden, and France. Half of the world's iron ore is produced in Europe. Bauxite is mined in the Soviet Union, France, Greece, and Hungary.

Above: Europe does not produce enough food to feed its population and much has to be imported. The export of manufactured goods pays for these imports. As a result, the harbours of Europe are among the busiest in the world.

countries have mild, wet winters and hot, dry summers. Eastern Europe has colder winters and short, hot summers.

Flora and Fauna

A large proportion of Europe's wild animals has been wiped out by the increasing human population and the spread of built-up areas. Survivors include wolves, bears, wild boars, beavers, elk, foxes, hares, and rabbits. The *chamois* (a species of antelope) makes its home in the Alps. Reindeer live in large herds in the northern forests. Birds are numerous, and include eagles, falcons, and storks.

Some parts of Europe are still thickly forested. Notable among these are Germany's Black Forest, and the plantations of olive and cork trees in the Mediterranean regions.

The People

The people of Europe are made up of a large number of different nationalities. They each have their own ways of life, languages, literatures, customs, and traditions. Today, Europe is divided into two main political regions: the 25 countries of Western Europe and the nine countries of Eastern or Communist Europe.

During the present century, Europe has had to recover from two world wars, mainly fought on its soil, and a number of smaller battles. As part of the postwar recovery, the European Economic Community was formed in 1957 by France, West Germany, Belgium, Italy, Luxembourg, and The Netherlands, and was joined in 1973 by Britain, Denmark, and the Republic of Ireland, and in 1981 by Greece.

Right: Population distribution map of Europe. The more dots on the map, the denser the population. More people live in the west and south than in the north and east.

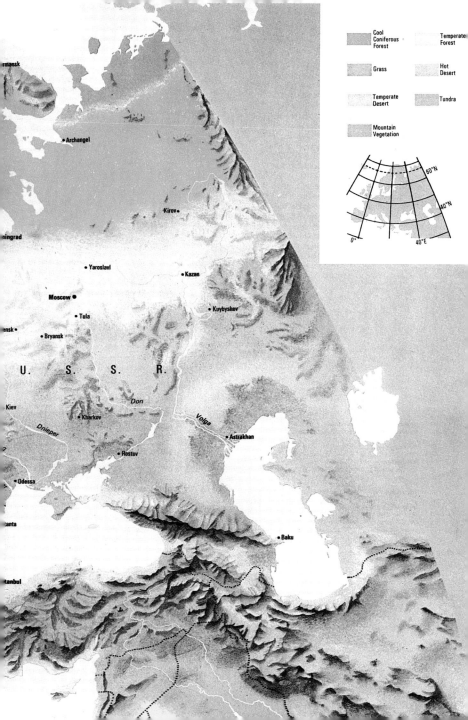

North America

North America is the third largest of the world's continents and occupies nearly a fifth of the Earth's land area. Only Asia and Africa are larger. Its physical limits are Panama in the south, and Alaska and Greenland in the north. Four-fifths of the continent are occupied by Canada and the United States, while the remainder is made up of Mexico and the small countries of Central America. There are also a large number of islands, the most important of which are the Caribbean Islands and Greenland, the world's largest. North America has an area of 24,390,000 km² (9,417,000 square miles). It has a population of more than 350 million.

Its land regions are fairly well marked. The Lawrentian region is an area of low-lying rocky land that stretches round Hudson Bay. It extends from the Arctic Ocean in the north to Labrador in the east.

The Appalachian region consists of a range of mountains running south-westwards from Quebec to Alabama. Bordering the Gulf of Mexico and the Atlantic Ocean, there are flat coastal

Above: The Niagara Falls frozen in winter. Below: Independence Hall, Philadelphia. The Declaration of Independence was signed here.

plains, including swamps.

To the west lie the great Western Highlands, known as the Cordilleras in Central America, and the Rocky Mountains in the rest of the continent. They stretch from Alaska to Central America. Running parallel to the Rockies are the Coast and Cascade ranges, and the Sierra Nevada.

The Great Plains form a 2,400-km (1,500-miles) wide belt, including part of central and northern Canada and the interior of the United States. These are grazing and grain-growing lands.

The Missouri-Mississippi river system in the heart of the continent is 5,900 km (3,700 miles) long, one of the longest in the world. The St. Lawrence

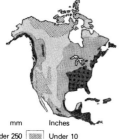

mm	Inches
Under 250	Under 10
250–500	10–20
500–1,000	20–40
1,000–2,000	40–80
Over 2,000	Over 80

The eastern half of North America has an annual rainfall between 500 and 1,800 mm (20–70 inches). The western half of the continent is semi-arid except for the Pacific coast.

January

July

Degrees C	Degrees F
Above 32	Above 90
21 to 32	70 to 90
10 to 21	50 to 70
−1 to 10	30 to 50
−18 to −1	−1 to 30
−34 to −18	−30 to −1
Below −34	Below −30

Over much of North America there is a wide range of seasonal temperatures. There are no mountain barriers to hinder southward movement of cold polar in the winter or the northward movement of hot air from the Gulf of Mexico in summer.

from the mosses and lichens that survive in the coldest regions of the Arctic, to the desert cactus of the waterless areas of the southwest. Trees include the redwoods and sequoias of California, the largest trees in the world, maples (whose leaf is the emblem of Canada), and tropical palms. Canada has enormous forests of fir, spruce, and pine.

Resources

In the United States and Canada there are vast tracts of fertile land, and the yield is constantly increasing because farmers use the latest equipment and methods. Canada exports more than half of its wheat to other countries.

North America has some of the world's richest deposits of minerals. The most important are coal,

River flows eastwards and connects the Great Lakes—Superior, Michigan, Huron, Erie, and Ontario—with the Atlantic.

The climate in the far south is always warm, and in the far north it is always cold. Annual rainfall varies from 3,500 mm (140 inches) in the Rockies to 38 mm (1½ inches) in the deserts.

Above: The White House in Washington, official residence of the President of the U.S.A.

Flora and Fauna

North America is still very rich in animal life, but as the population increases and spreads, the wildlife is rapidly disappearing from the continent. A hundred years ago the plains were filled with enormous herds of buffalo. Today, only a few herds remain. Nevertheless, the woods of central and eastern North America still hold black bears, deer, musquash, porcupines, and beavers. The Rockies are the home of eagles, grizzly bears, elk, and moose. In the far north are found some of the most valuable fur-bearing animals, including Arctic foxes, fur seals, and polar bears. Tropical creatures such as alligators, monkeys, jaguars, ant-eaters, and armadillos inhabit Central America.

North America's plant life varies

Below: A stone bowl made by American Indians in Mexico about A.D. 600.

A sacrificial knife with a chalcedony blade and wooden haft inlaid with turquoise and shell made by Aztec Indians in the 1400s.

petroleum, gold, iron, nickel, silver, lead, zinc, and copper. Both Canada and the United States are among the leading industrial nations of the world.

The People

Most of the people in the Latin American countries of the continent speak Spanish, but in the United States and Canada, English (with French in part of Canada) is the main language. The early settlers came mostly from Britain, France, and Spain, but in the United States there are people whose ancestors came from every European country, China and Japan. There are also Negroes, descended from African slaves, and some descendants of the original inhabitants, the North American Indians.

Above: Pulpwood logs and grain elevators in Ontario. Wheat, and paper made from wood, are two of Canada's major exports.

Left: A view of the New York skyline.

Below: The Canadian prairies are among the world's greatest wheat growing regions.

Above: Orange groves in Florida.

Right: Eskimoes inhabit the cold wastes of northern Canada. In recent years, many Eskimoes have left their old tribal life and become skilled workers.

60°N
20°N
140°W
100°W
60°W

0   400   800   1200   1600   2000 km

ARCTIC OCEAN

GREENLAND

HUDSON BAY

CANADA

Vancouver
Edmonton
Calgary
Winnipeg
Missouri
St. Lawrence
Québec
Ottawa • Montreal
Toronto
Minneapolis
Hamilton • Buffalo   Boston
Milwaukee   Detroit   NEW YORK
Chicago   Cleveland
San Francisco
Indianapolis   Pittsburgh   Philadelphia
Kansas City   Cincinnati   Baltimore
St. Louis   Washington
Los Angeles
Denver
Phoenix
Memphis
Atlanta
Rio Grande
Dallas
New Orleans   Mississippi
Houston
GULF OF MEXICO
Miami
MEXICO
Havana   CUBA   DOMINICAN   PUERTO
REPUBLIC   RICO
Mexico City
HAITI
GUATEMALA   JAMAICA
BELIZE
HONDURAS   CARIBBEAN SEA
NICARAGUA
COSTA RICA
PANAMA

PACIFIC OCEAN

ROCKY MOUNTAINS

U   S   A

ATLANTIC OCEAN

Cool
Coniferous
Forest

Temperate Forest

Tropical Forest

Equatorial Rain Forest

Grassland   Temperate Desert

Savanna   Tundra

Hot Desert   Mountain Vegetation

Africa

Africa is the world's second largest continent. With its area of 30,320,000 km² (11,671,000 square miles), it is three and a half times as large as the United States. But Africa has only twice the population of the United States—about 470,000,000 people.

Large parts of Africa are almost empty wasteland. Great, burning-hot deserts, including the Sahara in the north and the Namib and Kalahari in the south, cover about two-fifths of Africa. Life is only possible where water is available, near rivers such as the Nile in Egypt.

Near the Equator, especially in western and west-central Africa, the rainfall is very heavy, sometimes more than 3,800 mm (150 inches) a year. This hot, rain-drenched region is covered by thick, luxuriant forests.

Although most of Africa lies within the tropics, more than a third of the continent is a great *plateau* (high plain). Because they are so high, many parts of Africa close to the Equator have a pleasant climate. In eastern Africa are the continent's two highest mountains, Kilimanjaro in Tanzania (5,895 metres; 19,340 feet above sea level) and Mount Kenya (5,200 metres; 17,058 feet). Snow and ice cap the

Above: The baobab tree has an enormously thick trunk.
Below: The thousand-year-old ruined city of Zimbabwe has given its name to the country.

Below: The Zaïre is navigable by river boats for more than 1,600 km (1,000 miles).

peaks of these mountains.

Grassland called *savanna* covers much of the high plains of Africa. Great herds of animals still roam over Africa's grasslands and forests. In the past, thousands of animals were killed by hunters and poachers. To save the animals, many African governments have set up special parks and game reserves.

Throughout the eastern African plateau runs the deep African rift valley. This colossal valley stretches from Syria in Asia through the Red Sea and eastern Africa to Mozambique. It contains many lakes.

Africa's largest lake is Lake Victoria, which lies between Kenya and Tanzania. Its greatest rivers are the Nile, Zaïre (formerly Congo), Niger, and Zambesi.

People and Products

North of the Sahara, most of the people are Arabs or Berbers. Negroid Africans, who make up three-quarters of Africa's population, live south of the Sahara. More than five million people of European ancestry live in Africa, many of them in South Africa. Their ancestors were the pioneers who introduced western ideas of farming, mining, and industry. About half a millon people of Asian origin also live in Africa.

Above: Catching fish in bamboo traps at rapids on a tributary of the Zaïre River.

Key to Independent Countries and Dependencies

1, Algeria; 2, Botswana; 3, Burundi; 4, Cameroon; 5, Central African Republic; 6, Chad; 7, Congo; 8, Zaire; 9, Benin; 10, Egypt; 11, Equatorial Guinea; 12, Ethiopia; 13, Gabon; 14, Gambia; 15, Ghana; 16, Guinea; 17, Ivory Coast; 18, Kenya; 19, Lesotho; 20, Liberia; 21, Libya; 22, Madagascar (Malagasy Republic); 23, Malawi; 24, Mali; 25, Mauritania; 26, Mauritius; 27, Morocco; 28, Niger; 29, Nigeria; 30, Rwanda; 31, Senegal; 32, Sierra Leone; 33, Somalia; 34, South Africa; 35, Sudan; 36, Swaziland; 37, Tanzania; 38, Togo; 39, Tunisia; 40, Uganda; 41, Upper Volta; 42, Zambia; 43, Djibouti; 44, Angola; 45, Canary Islands (Spanish); 46, Cape Verde Islands; 47, Comoros; 48, Madeira Islands (Portuguese); 49, Mozambique; 50, Guinea-Bissau; 51, Réunion (French); 52, Zimbabwe; 53, St. Helena (British); 54, Sao Tomé and Principe; 55, Seychelles; 56, Namibia (South-West Africa).

Most Africans are farmers. They either rear cattle or grow crops to feed their families. The wealth of many African countries is based on one or two crops grown on plantations. Eastern Africa's main products are coffee and sisal. Africa produces nearly three-quarters of the world's palm oil and palm kernels. Other crops include cotton, fruits, tea, and tobacco.

Africa produces almost all the world's diamonds and a large quantity of gold. Other important minerals are copper, cobalt, petroleum, and uranium.

History

Northern Africa was important in the early growth of civilizations around the Mediterranean Sea. The Nile valley was the centre of one of the greatest early civilizations.

From the 1400s, European sailors began to ship slaves from Africa. The

Right: Berber woman from Morocco. The peoples north of the Sahara belong to the Caucasoid race.

Right: Washing clothes at an oasis. The Sahara contains many oases, ranging from mere water-holes to large fertile areas where many people live.

Below: Gold mining in South Africa.

Below: Negroid peoples inhabit most of Africa south of the Sahara. The Negroes of eastern and southern Africa have a lighter skin colour than the Negroes of western Africa.

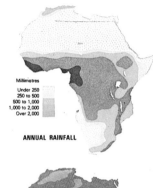

Millimetres
Under 250
250 to 500
500 to 1,000
1,000 to 2,000
Over 2,000

ANNUAL RAINFALL

°C
Above 32
21 to 32
10 to 21
Under 10

January Temperatures

July Temperatures

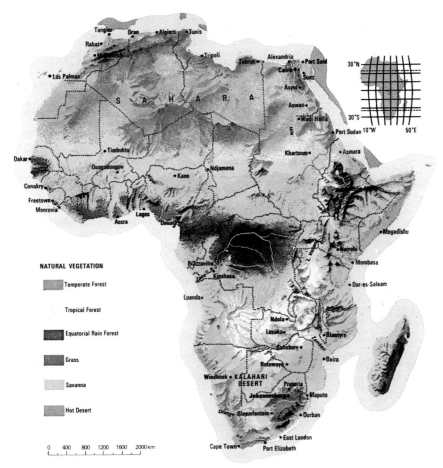

NATURAL VEGETATION

- Temperate Forest
- Tropical Forest
- Equatorial Rain Forest
- Grass
- Savanna
- Hot Desert

0   400   800   1200 1600 2000 km

slave trade continued until the 1800s. An estimated 14 million African slaves were shipped to the Americas. Usually the slave traders bought slaves from African coastal chiefs whose people raided inland tribes.

An early and important settlement at the Cape of Good Hope was established in 1652. This settlement developed to form part of present-day South Africa.

The great period of European exploration of the interior came during the 1800s. Many explorers were missionaries who helped to stamp out

Below: Herds of animals such as the giraffe are protected in game reserves.

the terrible slave trade. Information brought back by explorers interested European governments, who began to establish settlements and colonies. By the 1890s, almost all of Africa was divided up between the European powers.

From the 1890s to the 1950s, most African countries were European colonies. The Europeans introduced new ways of life and developed Africa. But many Africans resented foreign rule. Since the late 1950s almost all African countries have achieved independence.

Asia

Asia is the largest of the continents and has more people than any other continent. It covers 43,930,000 km² (16,961,000 square miles)—almost one-third of the land area of the world. Its population is about 2,444 million.

Asia is a continent of extremes. It has the highest mountains, the Himalayas, and the lowest depths, the shores of the Dead Sea, 395 metres (1,300 feet) below sea level. Parts of the continent are colder than the North Pole but other areas are among the hottest places on Earth. More rain falls in parts of southern Asia than anywhere else in the world, but some

The rivers of northern Asia empty into the Arctic Ocean. They freeze in winter. In spring, when their mouths are still blocked by ice, the rivers flood the land.

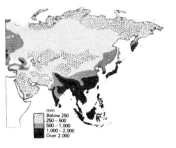

Stretching from the Arctic to the Equator, Asia has many contrasting climates. The rainfall varies from 1,140 mm (450 inches) a year in Assam to less than 25 mm (1 inch) in parts of the Gobi and Arabian deserts. Most of the rain in southern Asia falls during the summer months when monsoon winds blow on to the land.

Asia contains over half of the world's population. The map shows that the greatest concentration of people is in the broad river valleys of southern Asia.

Asian deserts are among the driest places on Earth.

Asia extends from the Ural Mountains in the west to the Pacific Ocean in the east; and from the Arctic Ocean in the north to the Indian Ocean in the south. Its south-western frontier with Europe runs along the shores of the Caspian Sea, Black Sea, and Mediterranean. Asia is joined to Africa by the isthmus of Suez. It is separated from North America by the Bering Strait in the north-east.

The Land

Asia can be conveniently divided into six major regions. Central or Inner Asia is a triangular mass of mountains and high, remote plateaux. It includes Tibet, Mongolia, and parts of western China. The Himalaya range includes Mt. Everest (8,848 metres; 29,028 feet), the world's highest peak.

Northern Asia includes the vast Russian lowlands of Siberia, and stretches from the Ural Mountains in the west to the Pacific Ocean in the east. It is drained by huge rivers. *Eastern Asia*, or the *Far East*, is a mountainous area that includes most of China, Japan, Korea, and Formosa.

Southern Asia lies to the south of the Himalayas. It includes the plateaux of Afghanistan, Bhutan, India, and Pakistan. *South-western Asia* is a dry region that includes Turkey, Iran, and the Arabian Peninsula. *South-eastern Asia* includes the land south of China and east of India, the Indonesian, Malaysian and Philippine islands, and Papua New Guinea.

Among Asia's important rivers are the Jordan, that flows southwards from Lebanon to the Dead Sea; the Tigris and Euphrates, which drain Iraq; the Brahmaputra and Ganges that empty into the Bay of Bengal; and the Indus, which rises in Tibet and flows into the Arabian Sea. China's chief rivers are Hwang, Si-Kiang, and Yangtze.

Flora and Fauna

Asian wild animals include tigers, monkeys, rhinoceroses, bears, deer, mongooses, and many kinds of poisonous and non-poisonous snakes.

Vegetation varies with the climate. Northern Asia contains the world's largest fir and pine forest. Temperate grasslands and desert scrub cover some other parts of the continent.

Resources and History

Most people in Asia eat rice as their main food. Rice grows in the wet, tropical regions. In drier areas other cereals such as maize, wheat, millet, and soya beans are grown. Timber is a valuable product. The tropical regions yield quantities of teak, pine wood comes from Siberia, and hardwoods from the forests of China. Other important agricultural products are tea, tobacco, rubber, dates, jute, cotton, and olives. About two-fifths of the world's petroleum comes from

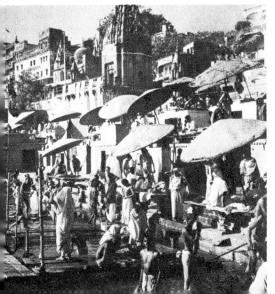

Top left: Every Burmese boy spends at least seven days in a Buddhist monastery during his early life. Bottom left: Hindus bathe in the Ganges, a river sacred to their faith.

Above: Cows are sacred to Hindus.

37

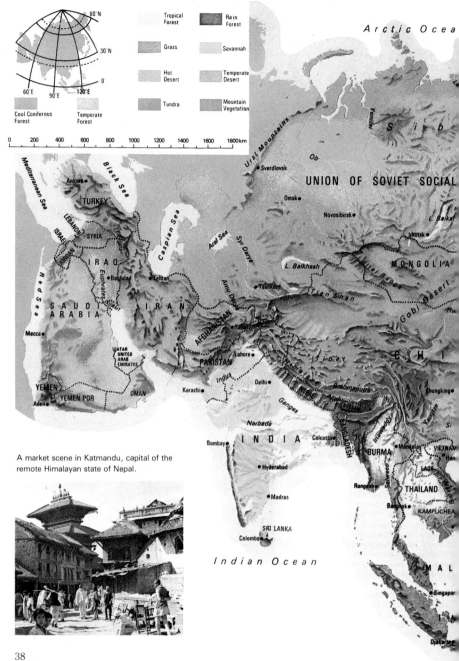

Tropical Forest
Grass
Hot Desert
Tundra
Cool Coniferous Forest
Temperate Forest
Rain Forest
Savannah
Temperate Desert
Mountain Vegetation

60°N
30°N
0°
60°E
90°E
120°E

| 0 | 200 | 400 | 600 | 800 | 1000 | 1200 | 1400 | 1600 | 1800km |

Arctic Ocea

Mediterranean Sea
Black Sea
Ankara
TURKEY
LEBANON
SYRIA
ISRAEL
JORDAN
IRAQ
Baghdad
Euphrates
KUWAIT
SAUDI ARABIA
Mecca
Red Sea
YEMEN
Aden
YEMEN PDR
OMAN
QATAR
UNITED ARAB EMIRATES
IRAN
Tehran
Caspian Sea
Aral Sea
Syr Darya
Amu Darya
Tashkent
L. Balkhash
Ural Mountains
Sverdlovsk
Ob
Omsk
Novosibirsk
UNION OF SOVIET SOCIAL
L. Baikal
Irkutsk
S i b
Yenisey
Altai Range
MONGOLIA
Tien Shan
Gobi Desert
AFGHANISTAN
Kabul
PAKISTAN
Lahore
Indus
Karachi
Delhi
Ganges
Narbada
Bombay
INDIA
Hyderabad
Madras
Calcutta
BANGLADESH
Brahmaputra
Himalayas
Tibet
Chungking
C H I
Si
Yangtze
BURMA
Mandalay
Irrawaddy
Salween
Rangoon
THAILAND
Bangkok
LAOS
VIETNAM
Han
KAMPUCHEA
M A L
Singapor
I N
Djakarta
SRI LANKA
Colombo
Indian Ocean

A market scene in Katmandu, capital of the remote Himalayan state of Nepal.

38

Above; Rice is the great cereal crop of Asia. The rice-fields must be flooded because rice grows in standing water.

Left: Independence Day celebrations in India. Since World War II many Asian nations have achieved independence.

Left: Street scene in Tokyo, the city claimed to have the largest population of any in the world. Below: In the hot, wet lands of southern Asia, people still build houses on stilts over rivers.

39

south-western Asia. Turkey and the Philippines export chromite, and nearly two-thirds of the world's tin comes from south-eastern Asia.

Much Asian industry consists of handicrafts produced in small factories and work-shops. The great exception is Japan, one of the most highly industrialized countries in the world. Northern China, parts of India, and central Siberia also have modern, well-equipped factories.

Most of the earliest civilizations and all the great religions began in Asia. Over 2,000 years ago powerful empires flourished in the continent. Their peoples reached a high development in the arts and sciences. They began to influence Europe, especially through contact with the ancient Greeks, from about 300 B.C.

Right: The main range of the mighty Himalaya mountains towers above the terraced foothills in Nepal. The Himalayas sweep in a great arc 2,400 km (1,500 miles) from the Pamir Knot in the west to the borders of China and Assam in the east.

Below: All the world's great religions began in Asia. The grotto at Bethlehem, the birthplace of Christ, is a hallowed shrine of Christendom.

Right (centre): In most parts of Asia articles are still handmade by individual craftsmen.

Right: Japan is one of the main exceptions. It is the industrial giant of Asia.

COUNTRIES OF ASIA	
Country	Capital
Afghanistan	Kabul
Bahrain	Manama
Bangladesh	Dacca
Bhutan	Thimpu
Brunei	Bandar Seri Begawan
Burma	Rangoon
China	Peking
Cyprus	Nicosia
India	New Delhi
Indonesia	Djakarta
Iran (Persia)	Tehran
Iraq	Baghdad
Israel	Jerusalem
Japan	Tokyo
Jordan	Amman
Kampuchea (Cambodia)	Phnom Penh
Korea, North	Pyongyang
Korea, South	Seoul
Kuwait	Kuwait
Laos	Vientiane
Lebanon	Beirut
Malaysia	Kuala Lumpur
Maldives	Malé
Mongolia	Ulan Bator
Nepal	Katmandu
Oman	Muscat
Pakistan	Islamabad
Papua New Guinea	Port Moresby
Philippines	Quezon City
Qatar	Doha
Saudi Arabia	Riyadh
Singapore	Singapore
Soviet Union	Moscow
Sri Lanka (Ceylon)	Colombo
Syria	Damascus
Taiwan	Taipei
Thailand (Siam)	Bangkok
Turkey (Asiatic)	Ankara
United Arab Emirates	Abu Dhabi
Vietnam	Hanoi
Yemen	San'a
Yemen PDR	Aden

South America

South America is the fourth largest continent, covering 13 per cent of the Earth's land area. It is almost twice the size of the United States, but is sparsely populated.

South America is joined to Central and North America by the Isthmus of Panama, and lies almost entirely to the east of them. It has an area of 17,829,000 km² (6,870,000 square miles), and a population of around 240,000,000, increasing rapidly.

The Land and Climate

The land can be divided into three main regions running north and south: in the west, the Andes, running parallel to the Pacific coastline; in the centre, the great central plains, stretching from the Orinoco Basin to Patagonia; and in the east, the eastern highlands.

The Andes rise to more than 6,000 metres (20,000 feet) in places, and stretch from Panama to Tierra del Fuego in the south. The plains in the centre of the continent go by various names, according to their latitude. In the north, on the borders of the Guianas and Brazil, they form the Llanos. The Brazilian jungles are

Above: Simón Bolívar liberated several South American countries from Spanish rule.

Above: Spreading coffee beans to dry in the sun. South America produces nearly half the world's coffee.

Below: Brasília, the futuristic capital of Brazil, was built in the 1950s and 1960s.

called *selvas*. Farther south, the *Gran Chaco,* a vast region of grasslands, swamps, and lakes, stretches across parts of Bolivia, Paraguay, and Argentina. From the Gran Chaco to Patagonia in the far south are the *pampas,* the farming and grazing lands from which Argentina gets most of its wealth.

The eastern highlands are much lower than the Andes. They consist of the Guiana Highlands, the Brazilian Highlands and the Patagonian Plateau.

South America's river system is dominated in the north by the immense Amazon basin. In the north-west, the rivers Magdalena and Cauca join in the north of Colombia and empty into the Caribbean Sea. The Orinoco, fed by more than 400 tributaries, flows through the middle of Venezuela into the Atlantic Ocean. The eastern Brazilian Highlands are drained by the Sao Francisco that also flows into the Atlantic. The most important waterway system in South America is the Río de la Plata. This is a broad estuary formed by the rivers Paraná, Paraguay, and Uruguay.

Most of South America lies within the tropics, and its climate is generally warm and sunny throughout the year. In the Brazilian jungles, on the Equator, it is always hot and humid. High in the Andes the snow never melts. In the south, summers (December to March) are cool, and winters (June to September) are mild. The heaviest rainfall (more than 1,500 mm; 60 inches a year) occurs in the Amazon valley, the coasts of the Guianas, Colombia, and Ecuador, and in south-western Chile. But strips of northern Chile and Peru, and Patagonia get practically no rainfall, and are virtually deserts. The icy Peru Current of the Pacific Ocean swirls along the coasts of Chile and Peru and keeps them cool.

Flora and Fauna

Although about a quarter of all the world's known animals live in South

Caribbean Sea

Barranquilla
Cartagena
Maracaibo
Valencia
Caracas
Port of Spain
Barquisimeto
Cúcuta
Bucaramanga
Orinoco
Georgetown
Paramaribo
Cayenne
VENEZUELA
GUYANA
SURINAM
FRENCH GUIANA
Medellín
Bogotá
COLOMBIA
Cali
Quito
ECUADOR
Guayaquil
Amazon
Belém
Fortaleza

ATLANTIC
OCEAN

B R A Z I L

João
Recife
Maceió

Callao
Lima
Salvador
PERU
BOLIVIA
Arequipa
La Paz
Paraguay
Brasília
Paraná
Belo Horizonte

PACIFIC
OCEAN

PARAGUAY
Rio de Janeiro
São Paulo
Santos
Niterói
Asunción
Coritiba

Tucumán

Porto Alegre
Córdoba
Santa Fé
Paraná
URUGUAY
Mendoza
Rosario
Valparaíso
Santiago
Buenos Aires
Montevideo
La Plata
Concepción
CHILE
Mar del Plata
Bahía Blanca

ARGENTINA

| | |
|10°N|
|0°|
|10°S|
|30°S|
|50°S|
80°W 60°W 40°W

0   400   800   1200   1600   2000 km

Temperate Forest

Tropical Forest

Equatorial
Rain Forest

Grassland

Savanna

Hot Desert

Temperate Desert

Tundra

Mountain Vegetation

FALKLAND IS.
Stanley

42

America, there are no large herds of game such as are found in North America and Africa. Most of the animals are found in the rain forests of the Amazon Basin. The largest animal in South America is the tapir, which is about the size of a small pony. Some 2,500 kinds of trees flourish in South America's rain forests.

People and Products

South America is part of a larger cultural region called *Latin America*. This includes nearly all of Central America, Mexico, some Caribbean islands, and the whole of South America, with the exception of Surinam and French Guiana. Latin America was discovered and explored by Spanish and Portuguese adven-

Above: Population distribution map of South America. The heart of the continent is the sparsely populated Amazon Basin.

turers in the 1500s.

There are 12 independent countries in South America. The largest is Brazil, the smallest is Guyana. In addition, French Guiana (an overseas department of France) occupies the north-east coast of the continent. The people are descended from European settlers (mostly Spanish and Portuguese), the American Indians who lived there before the Europeans arrived, and Negro slaves imported to work on the plantations. All these peoples have intermarried.

Over a third of the people of South America are farmers. Although manufacturing is growing rapidly, many manufactured articles have still to be imported.

Right: The ruins of Machu Picchu, a fortress city of an ancient American Indian nation, the Incas.

A Bolivian boy partly descended from American Indians.

Below: The sturdy llama is used as a pack animal in the Andes.

Temperature

January

°C	°F
21–32	70–90
10–21	50–70
Minus 1–10	30–50
Under Minus 1	Under 30

July

Annual Rainfall

inches	mm
Under 10	Under 250
10–20	250–500
20–40	500–1,000
40–80	1,000–2,000
Over 80	Over 2,000

New Zealand

New Zealand is a Pacific Ocean country lying about 1,600 km (1,000 miles) south-east of Australia. Most of New Zealand is made up of two large islands, called North Island and South Island. It contains several other islands, but they are very small.

North Island, where two-thirds of all New Zealanders live, has low mountains and hills which include active volcanoes and warm springs. South Island is separated from North Island by the narrow Cook Strait. From the Strait, the Southern Alps stretch south-westwards for more than 800 km (500 miles). New Zealand's highest mountain, Mount Cook, rises from this range.

New Zealand has a mild climate. In January the country's mid-summer temperature averages about 20°C (68°F). In July, temperatures drop to about 6°C (4°F). Rainfall is very varied, averaging between 500 and 5,000 mm (20–200 inches) in various parts of the islands.

Above: A sheep-shearer at work. Meat and wool are important New Zealand exports.

Right: Cattle are important in New Zealand and butter is a major export.

Below: The city and harbour of Wellington, the capital.

New Zealand has several species of rare birds. The tail-less kiwi is often used as a symbol for the country.

People and Resources

About seven peoole out of every 100 are *Maoris*, who are descendants of the Polynesian people who sailed to the islands about 700 years ago. The rest are descended from British and Irish settlers, or are themselves from the British Isles. Many marriages have occurred between Maoris and Europeans. The official language of New Zealand is English, but the Maoris also speak their own language.

New Zealand was one of the earliest countries to introduce social reforms and a social security system, including old age pensions.

History

The earliest-known people in New Zealand were Moriois—a Polynesian people. They were conquered in about the 1300s by another Polynesian people, Maoris, who settled mainly on the coastal parts of North Island.

Abel Tasman, commander of a ship sailing for the Dutch East India Company, sighted New Zealand in 1642. The Dutch named the islands after Zeeland, a province in the Netherlands. The British began colonising the country in 1839.

In 1840, Maori chiefs signed a treaty accepting British rule, and in 1841 New Zealand became a colony independent of Australia. Disputes about land led to war between the Maoris and the settlers in 1845–1848. Fighting occurred again in the 1860s and 1870s. In 1907, New Zealand became an independent dominion within the British Commonwealth.

Half of New Zealand's area is farmland, and the country exports butter, lamb, fruit and other food products. Farmers grow cereals for consumption in New Zealand. Because the most modern methods of farming are used, only an eighth of the country's people work on the land. Over a third of the people work in manufacturing and processing industries of various kinds. Much electrical power comes from hydroelectric plants, which harness the power of New Zealand's rushing rivers.

Forests cover over a quarter of New Zealand. The country's mineral wealth includes coal, iron ore, gold, limestone, natural gas, silver, and tungsten.

A Maori girl shows visitors around Pohutu geyser at Rotorua, North Island.

NEW ZEALAND

North Cape

Temperate Forest

Grass

Railways

Auckland

Hamilton

Rotorua

NORTH ISLAND

Gisborne

New Plymouth

Napier

Hastings

Palmerston North

Cook Strait

Nelson

Wellington

SOUTH PACIFIC OCEAN

TASMAN SEA

Christchurch

Lyttelton

SOUTH ISLAND

SOUTHERN ALPS

CANTERBURY PLAINS

Timaru

No. of rainy days per year

Less than 125

125-175

More than 175

LAND USE

Sheep

Mixed Farming

Dairying

Forests

Dunedin

Invercargill

Stewart Island

45

Australia

Australia is a country that is also a continent. It lies in the southern hemisphere. It is about three-quarters of the size of Europe, but Europe has 33 times as many people.

Several islands lie around the coast. The largest and most important of these is Tasmania, which is south of the mainland of Australia. The Great Barrier Reef on the north-eastern coast is a 1,900-km (1,200-mile) chain of coral reefs and islets.

Most of the western and central part of Australia is a high flat plateau. Few people live there. The eastern third of the continent is more varied. Close to the east coast is a long range of mountains, called the Great Dividing Range. The highest mountain is Mount Kosciusko (2,230 metres; 7,316 feet).

Right: An aerial view of Sydney, the capital of New South Wales and Australia's largest city.

Right: The koala, a small, furry, pouched mammal of eastern Australia, feeds on the leaves of the eucalyptus tree.

Left: Australia has about 135,000,000 sheep—nine for every inhabitant—and produces more than one-quarter of the world's wool. Australia is also the second largest exporter of mutton and lamb.

Left: Annual rainfall map of Australia. More than one-third of the entire continent receives less than 250 mm (10 inches) of rain each year.

Right: Tuna fishing off the coast of New South Wales.

mm	inches
Under 250	10
250–500	10–20
500–1,000	20–40
1,000–2,000	40–80
Over 2,000	Over 80

January Temperatures   July Temperatures

°F

Below 30   30–50   50–70   70–90   Over 90°F

STATES AND TERRITORIES OF AUSTRALIA

State or Territory	Area (sq. km.)	Area (sq. mi.)	Capital
Australian Capital Territory	2,432	939	Canberra
New South Wales	801,428	309,433	Sydney
Northern Territory	1,347,519	520,280	Darwin
Queensland	1,727,522	667,000	Brisbane
South Australia	984,377	380,070	Adelaide
Tasmania	68,332	26,383	Hobart
Victoria	227,619	87,884	Melbourne
Western Australia	2,527,621	975,920	Perth

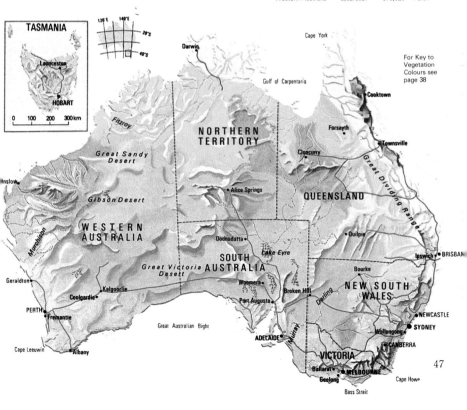

For Key to Vegetation Colours see page 38

TASMANIA

Launceston

HOBART

0   100   200   300km

120°E   140°E
20°S
40°S

Cape York

Darwin

Gulf of Carpentaria

Cooktown

Fitzroy

NORTHERN TERRITORY

Forsayth

Townsville

Great Sandy Desert

Cloncurry

Great Dividing Range

Onslow

Gibson Desert

Alice Springs

QUEENSLAND

WESTERN AUSTRALIA

Oodnadatta

Quilpie

Murchison

Lake Eyre

SOUTH AUSTRALIA

Ipswich   BRISBANE

Geraldton

Great Victoria Desert

Woomera

Bourke

NEW SOUTH WALES

Coolgardie   Kalgoorlie

Broken Hill

Darling

PERTH   Fremantle

Port Augusta

Great Australian Bight

Murray

NEWCASTLE

Cape Leeuwin   Albany

ADELAIDE

Wollongong   SYDNEY

CANBERRA

VICTORIA

Ballarat   MELBOURNE

Geelong   Cape Howe

Bass Strait

47

Above: The sail-shaped roof of the Sydney Opera House is a striking feature of the city.

Below: The kookaburra, or laughing jackass, found in southern and eastern Australia, is famed for its unusual call—a full-throated laugh ending in a short chuckle.

Below: Intricate coral formations make up the Great Barrier Reef.

The northern part of Australia lies in the tropics, just north of the Tropic of Capricorn. Along the coast, it is hot and wet, with heavy rains every year. South-eastern and south-western Australia have hot, dry summers and warm, moist winters.

Most of the centre of the country has very unreliable rainfall. In some years, rain may fall, but several years of drought may follow.

Australia is rich in minerals, including bauxite, coal, copper, gold, iron, lead, nickel, silver, tin, uranium, and zinc. Petroleum and natural gas have been found off the coasts. Huge underground stores of water lie under parts of the country called Artesian Basins.

Australia has a number of kinds of animals of its own. They include *marsupials*, which are animals with pouches. The biggest are the kangaroos. The duck-billed platypus, a mammal which lays eggs, is another unique Australian animal.

The People

Most of the people of Australia are of British origin. Since World War II more than three and a half million people from Europe have emigrated to Australia. In addition, there are about 136,300 Aborigines, whose ancestors were the first inhabitants of Australia.

More than half the people of Australia live in cities. The rest live in small towns or villages, or in lonely farms called *stations*.

Mining and manufacturing provide more than two-thirds of Australia's wealth. The rest is provided by farming. The country exports great quantities of wool and wheat. It also has many cattle and produces much butter and cheese.

Australia is a *federation* or group of separate states, with a central government linking them together. Australia has six states: New South Wales, Queensland, South Australia, Tasmania, Victoria, and Western Australia. Each state has its own parliament. Northern Territory and the Australian Capital Territory come under the direct rule of the central government.

History

The first people to occupy Australia were the Aborigines. They arrived in the continent about 20,000 years ago.

Australia was visited by Abel Tasman and other Dutch explorers in the early 17th century, and at first it was called New Holland. Then, in 1770 the British explorer Captain James Cook landed in Botany Bay, on the south-eastern coast, and claimed it for Britain.

From 1788 the British used the new territory as a *penal settlement*—a kind of open prison where criminals could be sent, guarded by a few soldiers. But many other people settled there, too.

Gold was discovered in New South Wales and Victoria in.1851. During the next ten years about 700,000 people flocked to Australia to look for gold. The transportation of convicts had ceased by 1867. Australia became an independent country in 1901 as the *Commonwealth of Australia.*

During World War I, Australian troops fought in Europe against the Germans. During World War II, they fought in northern Africa and against the Japanese in New Guinea. In the past 50 years Australia has grown greatly in population and wealth.

The Polar Regions

The polar regions are those parts of the world which lie within the Arctic and Antarctic Circles (these correspond to latitudes 66c° North and South). Everywhere within these circles there is at least one day during summer when the Sun does not set, and at least one day during the winter when the Sun does not rise. At the poles themselves there are six months of continual day and six months of continual night. The long polar 'night' is not as dark as it sounds, for the reflected moonlight is often bright enough to read by.

Right: Eskimo hunter from Greenland dressed in Caribou and Polar Bear fur.

The Arctic

The northern polar region includes the Arctic Ocean, which has an area of about 14,100,000 km² (5,444,000 square miles). During the winter, pack-ice covers most of the Arctic Ocean. The ice is continually in motion, and as it grinds together large pressure ridges form. In the spring the ice begins to melt around the edges. Stretches of water appear between the ice floes.

Large parts of Asia and North America and a small part of Europe lie within the Arctic Circle. Some regions are covered with snow and ice the whole year round but other areas, called the *tundra*, are only covered with snow for two-thirds of the year.

Reindeer and caribou graze in the Arctic in summer, but travel south in winter. Other animals include bears, ermine and foxes.

The Eskimos are perhaps the most famous of all Arctic dwellers. They inhabit a broad region from the Bering Strait to Baffin Island and southern Greenland.

The Antarctic

The only land within the Antarctic Circle is Antarctica, the coldest, windiest, loneliest and most desolate continent of all. It is about twice the

Above: In winter, when other penguins leave for the open sea, the Emperor penguin stays to rear its solitary chick.

size of Australia and is almost entirely shrouded in snow and ice the whole year round.

There are no flowering plants, but a few mosses and lichens cling to patches of bare rock along the coast. The animal life consists of wingless insects, sea birds and seals, but in the summer millions of noisy penguins come to Antarctica and gather in large 'rookeries'. The only people living in Antarctica are groups of scientists managing scientific stations.

Right: The Antarctic is inhospitable and dangerous but it can be dramatically beautiful.

The Animal Kingdom

Biologists know well over a million different species (kinds) of animals. Animals vary from the tiny one-celled amoeba—so small that it can be seen only under a microscope—to the huge blue whale, which may reach a length of 30 metres (100 feet).

One important difference between plants and animals is that most animals have far more accurate and sensitive senses. They can learn more precisely what is happening in their surroundings, and react quickly to it. This is because they have some kind of nervous system. Most animals can also move about.

In spite of their great variety, most animals have similar features to some other animals. Biologists use such

Above: Female *Anopheles* mosquito, the carrier of malaria. Man wages a continual battle against insect pests of this kind. Insects are one of the most successful groups of animals. There are about one million known kinds, more than all other species of animals added together.

Below: A family tree of the Animal Kingdom.

similarities to classify animals into groups. The closer they are related—the more similar—the closer the grouping. In this way, a number of species may be grouped into a single *genus*, several of which make up a *family*. Families are grouped into *orders*. A number of orders make a *class*; several classes comprise a *phylum*. The phyla make up the animal *kingdom*.

Perhaps the most varied and most important phylum is the *Chordata*, the chordates. What distinguishes them from all other animals is the hollow nerve cord that extends the length of their backs. They also have some kind of supporting rod of elastic material. Vertebrates are the most advanced and successful of the chordates, and include fishes, amphibians, reptiles, birds, and mammals. Man belongs to the mammal group.

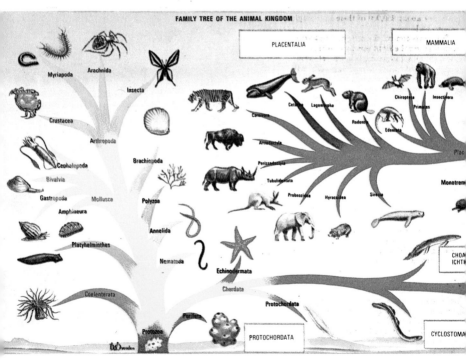

FAMILY TREE OF THE ANIMAL KINGDOM

PLACENTALIA

MAMMALIA

Myriapoda
Arachnida
Insecta
Crustacea
Arthropoda
Cephalopoda
Bivalvia
Gastropoda
Mollusca
Amphineura
Brachiopoda
Polyzoa
Annelida
Platyhelminthes
Nematoda
Echinodermata
Chordata
Coelenterata
Protochordata
Porifera
Protozoa

Carnivora
Cetacea
Lagomorpha
Chiroptera
Insectivora
Primates
Rodentia
Edentata
Artiodactyla
Perissodactyla
Tubulidentata
Proboscidea
Hyracoidea
Sirenia
Plac
Monotrem
CHOA
ICHTH
CYCLOSTOMA

PROTOCHORDATA

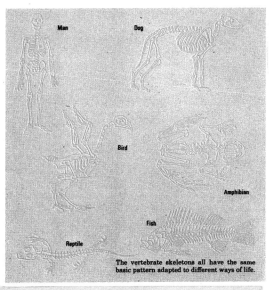

The vertebrate skeletons all have the same basic pattern adapted to different ways of life.

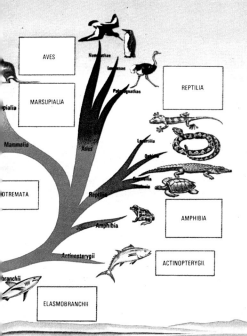

THE CHORDATES

Protochordata Animals with no true brain or backbone. They include sea-squirts.

Cyclostomata Jawless sea-animals with a skeleton of cartilage (gristle). They include lampreys and hagfishes.

Elasmobranchii Fishes with jaws and a skeleton of cartilage — sharks and rays.

Choanichthyes Fishes with internal nostrils. Examples include coelacanth and lungfishes.

Actinopterygii Ray-finned fishes with bony skeletons, including all the common fishes.

Amphibia Cold-blooded animals that breed in water but spend some time on land. They include frogs, toads, newts, and salamanders.

Reptilia Cold-blooded, land-living animals, with scaly skin. They include crocodiles, turtles, snakes, and lizards.

Aves The birds, warm-blooded animals with feathers and wings.

Mammalia Animals which nourish their young on milk from mammary glands.

Monotremata Mammals which lay eggs — the platypus and the spiny ant-eater.

Marsupialia Mammals with marsupia (pouches), to carry the young; including kangaroos.

Placentalia Mammals in which the unborn young are connected to the mother by a placenta, a 'plate' of tissue.

Insectivora Primitive insect-eating animals.

Primates Mostly tree-dwelling animals, including monkeys, apes, and Man.

Chiroptera Bats, the only mammals capable of powered flight; a few others can glide.

Edentata Animals with few or no teeth. They include sloths and armadillos.

Rodentia Animals with one pair of gnawing teeth in each jaw. They include rats, mice, squirrels, and beavers.

Lagomorpha Rabbits and hares, with two pairs of gnawing teeth in the upper jaw and one pair in the lower jaw.

Cetacea Whales, dolphins, and porpoises, mammals which live entirely in the sea.

Carnivora Flesh-eating animals — dogs, cats, bears, seals.

Artiodactyla Even-toed hoofed animals — cattle, pigs, deer, sheep, camels, goats.

Perissodactyla Odd-toed hoofed animals — horses, tapirs, rhinoceroses.

Tubulidentata The aardvark, an animal with peg-like teeth.

Proboscidea Animals with a trunk and tusks — the elephants.

Hyracoidea Hyraxes, small hoofed mammals with gnawing teeth.

Pholidota The scaly pangolins.

Sirenia Plant-eating sea-mammals — manatees, sea-cows, and dugongs.

The Insect World

Insects include animals such as butterflies, bees, beetles, grasshoppers, dragonflies, and earwigs. They all belong to a large group of creatures called *arthropods*, which have jointed legs and the whole body encased in a tough coat. This coat is an external skeleton, rather like a suit of armour, with joints to allow movement. If you look carefully at an insect you will see that it has three parts to the body, three pairs of jointed legs, and one pair of feelers or antennae. Most insects also have one or two pairs of wings.

Nobody knows just how many different kinds of insects there are. About a million different kinds have already been found and more are being discovered every day. There are enormous numbers of most kinds of insects.

Very few insects have managed to invade the sea, but they live almost everywhere on the land and in fresh water. They are certainly a very successful group of animals. But what

Above: A scarab beetle rolling a ball of dung with its hind legs. An egg laid in the dung develops into a grub which feeds inside the ball (shown cut open).

Above: The male (top left), queen (top right), soldier (bottom left), and worker (bottom right) of the harvesting ant. Each kind of ant has its own work in the ant community.

makes them so numerous and successful? The ability to fly obviously helps because it enables the insects to spread themselves rapidly from place to place. A rapid breeding rate also helps them to spread quickly. But one of the most important reasons for their success is their small size. The heaviest insect weighs only about 115 g (4 oz), while most of them are very much smaller and some cannot be seen without a magnifying glass.

Breathing and Feeding

The small size of insect bodies is controlled partly by their method of breathing. We breathe by taking air into our lungs and then carrying the oxygen around our bodies in our blood. Insects have no lungs, however, and they breathe in a very different way. Along the sides of the insect there are a number of small holes called *spiracles*, most easily seen in large caterpillars. The spiracles lead to tiny tubes called *tracheae* which spread through the body. Air seeps along these tubes to supply the insect with oxygen.

The small size of insects enables

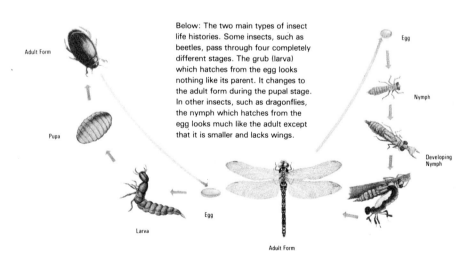

Below: The two main types of insect life histories. Some insects, such as beetles, pass through four completely different stages. The grub (larva) which hatches from the egg looks nothing like its parent. It changes to the adult form during the pupal stage. In other insects, such as dragonflies, the nymph which hatches from the egg looks much like the adult except that it is smaller and lacks wings.

Adult Form

Pupa

Larva

Egg

Egg

Nymph

Developing Nymph

Adult Form

them to inhabit places and use food supplies which could not possibly support larger animals. Many insects spend their lives tunnelling between the upper and lower surfaces of leaves. Some insects spend most of their lives inside the eggs of other insects.

Wood, blood, hair, wax, dung, and mould are some of the unusual things eaten by insects in addition to the more usual diets of plants and other animals. The ability to use so many different foods is another reason why the insects are such a successful group.

The mouths of insects are designed for their various diets. Beetles and grasshoppers feed on solid materials and they possess strong jaws for cutting and chewing their food. Butterflies and moths suck nectar from flowers and their mouths are drawn out into long 'tongues' which they push into the flowers. When the 'tongue' is not being used it is rolled up under the head. Blood-sucking insects, such as fleas and mosquitos, have needle-like jaws which puncture the skin and form a channel for blood to flow into the mouth. Sap-sucking insects, such as greenfly, have similar mouths.

Insect Life Histories

The tough outer skeleton of an insect does not grow with the animal and it has to be replaced by a larger one at intervals. This coat-changing is called *moulting* and it takes place between two and fifty times during the insect's life. Four or five moults are most common. When the young insect's coat has become too tight, the insect rests for a short while and then puffs itself up with air (or water if it lives in water). This splits the old coat but a new and larger one has grown underneath. The insect wriggles out of the old skin and soon the new soft skin hardens.

There are two main types of life history among insects, one in which the young looks something like the adult and one in which the young does not

Above: Some wasps make nests of clay (top). Others make nests of paper (middle). A section through a paper nest (bottom) shows the cells in which the eggs are laid.

look anything like the adult. The grasshopper has the first type of life history. The young grasshopper looks like the adult except that it is smaller and has no wings. At each moult the grasshopper gets larger and so do its wings. After the final moult the wings are fully formed.

The second type of life history is best seen in butterflies. The young butterfly looks nothing like a butterfly at all and is called a caterpillar. It has biting jaws and it eats leaves instead of drinking nectar. When it moults it gets bigger, but there is no sign of wings. The creature remains a caterpillar until it reaches full size. Then it changes into a *pupa* or *chrysalis*. The pupa does not move about, and inside it the caterpillar's body is converted into a butterfly. The adult butterfly then breaks out of the pupa skin and, after its wings have hardened, it flies away.

Most insects lead solitary lives. A few insects, however, live in large family groups, with each member doing a certain job. These are the *social* insects, which include the termites, ants, and some bees and wasps.

Below: A bush cricket, one of the long-horned grasshoppers which chirp by rubbing their wing covers together.

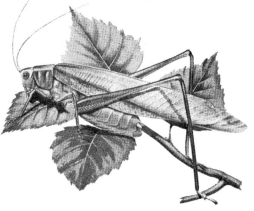

Ulysses' Butterfly
(Australia, New Guinea)

The Monarch or Milkweed
(Widespread)

The Zebra
(North America)

The Brimstone
(Europe)

The Small Copper or American Copper
(North America, Europe)

The Smoky Orange Tip
(Africa)

The Fiery Acrea
(Africa)

The Zebra Swallowtail
(North America)

Kahukura or Rainbow Butterfly
(New Zealand)

The Camberwell Beauty
(Europe, North America)

The Regent Skipper
(Australia)

The Adonis Blue
(Europe)

The Silver Barred Charaxes
(Africa)

The Birdwing
(Australia, New Guinea)

Butterflies are the most beautiful of insects. Like moths, butterflies have large wings, often with brilliant colours and striking patterns. The colours come from minute scales which cover the wings. It is not always easy to tell butterflies and moths apart, but, as a general rule, moths fly at night and butterflies during the day. Also, a butterfly usually holds its wings upright when it alights on a flower, whereas a moth usually spreads its wings out flat.

Camouflage and Mimicry

Many insects are camouflaged, which helps to save them from being eaten by birds and other enemies. Some moths, for example, are just the same colour as the tree trunks on which they rest and they become almost invisible when they settle. Some insects resemble objects in their surroundings, and include a moth that looks like a bird dropping, plant hoppers that look like prickles, and stick and leaf insects.

Not all insects are camouflaged, however. Some are brightly coloured and stand out clearly. Insects like this are usually poisonous or unpleasant to

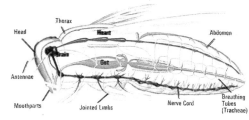

Above: The generalized body-plan of an insect. The body consists of three main regions: the head, thorax, and abdomen. The thorax usually bears wings and three pairs of walking legs. The head bears a single pair of feelers (antennae) and jointed mouthparts.

Left: The body of a typical insect (a bee) viewed from above.

Right: The common housefly is a dangerous insect pest. It spreads disease by transferring to fresh food germs picked up on previous visits to animal dung and rotting vegetation.

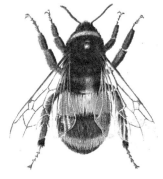

taste, and the bright colours or bold patterns warn their enemies to keep away. Quite often a harmless species looks like a poisonous one with warning colours. The harmless one benefits from this resemblance, or *mimicry*, because birds will think it is poisonous and avoid it. For example, hoverflies look like poisonous wasps.

Insects and Man

Many insects are a great nuisance to us because they eat our food, our clothes, and even our houses. They also carry diseases which affect us, our animals, and our crops. But not all insects are harmful, and some of them are extremely useful to us. One of the most useful is the honey bee which provides honey and also pollinates many plants.

Without the bees' aid, the plants could not produce fruits and seeds. Wasps are useful, too. Young wasps are fed on small insects and a single wasp nest will account for thousands of garden pests. The silkworm is another very useful insect. It is really the caterpillar of a moth and it wraps itself in a silken cocoon before turning into a pupa. Many caterpillars do this, but they do not make such good silk as the silkworm and nearly all the world's silk comes from this insect.

Right: A selection of insects showing the wide variety of forms which is to be found among this group of animals.

Spiders

Like insects, spiders belong to the group called *arthropods*, with jointed legs and tough outer skeletons. But unlike insects they have two parts to their body instead of three; four pairs of legs instead of three; and no antennae. They are the most important members of the *Arachnida*, which also includes scorpions, mites, and harvestmen.

All spiders can produce strands of silk from their bodies, from which many of them spin webs. Perfectionists in the art of web-spinning are the members of the *Argiopidae* family such as the garden spiders. Their cartwheel webs, composed of radiating strands connected by cross-threads, form a delicate drape over windows and hedges.

When its web is complete, the spider rests in the centre, or hides at the edge. But it remains in contact with the web by means of a thread, and quickly senses vibrations caused by a trapped insect. Then the spider rushes out and wraps its victim in fresh silk, biting it once or twice in the process (all spiders have poison fangs with which to paralyse their prey).

By no means all spiders spin webs. The wolf spider runs down its prey with a tremendous burst of speed. Some wolf spiders are inconspicuous, scurrying creatures, but one is probably the most famous spider of all—the tarantula. Despite all the legends, the bite of a tarantula is not deadly to human beings. Spiders which really are dangerous are those of the genus *Latrodectus*, such as the black widow of America. The bite of this spider is by no means always fatal, but it is extremely painful.

Above: Spiders belong to the Arachnid group which also includes scorpions. Arachnids have four pairs of walking legs. A scorpion, such as the one shown at the bottom right above, also has a large pair of jaws (chelicerae); the jaws of spiders are much smaller. Many spiders build webs in which to catch their prey. When a 'cartwheel' web is touched, the spider rushes out of hiding and moves to the centre of the web.

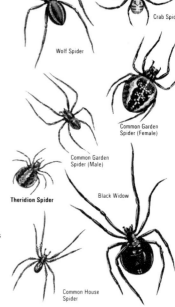

Crab Spider

Wolf Spider

Common Garden Spider (Female)

Common Garden Spider (Male)

Theridion Spider

Black Widow

Common House Spider

Right: Some members of the spider group. The Black Widow can inflict an extremely painful bite.

Fishes

Fishes are cold-blooded animals—their bodies take on the temperature of the water surrounding them. They are found all over the world.

Fishes can be grouped into *freshwater* and *salt-water* fishes. But as some fishes can live in both kinds of water, scientists prefer to classify fishes by their body structure into three classes. The majority of fishes are *bony* fishes—they have skeletons made of bone. The *cartilaginous* fishes—sharks, skates, and rays—have skeletons of cartilage, a gristly substance. The lampreys and hagfish are jawless fishes with cartilaginous skeletons.

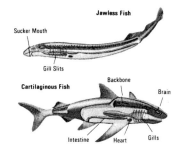

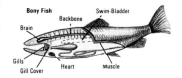

Fins and Scales

A fish moves through the water by bending its body to and fro, and by moving its tail. The *dorsal* fins, along the topside of the body, and the *anal* fin, on the underside just in front of the tail, help to keep the fish on an even keel. The two *pelvic* fins in the middle of the underside and the pair of *pectoral* fins just behind the head control vertical movement and also act as brakes. Turning movements are controlled by the tail and the pectoral fins.

Most fishes are covered with scales. In most bony fishes, there is a line of special scales along the middle of the body. This line is called the *lateral line*, and through these scales a fish can sense vibrations in the water.

Internal Organs

The fish's internal organs are similar to those of other backboned animals. Bony fishes have an additional body organ to those of other animals: the *swim-bladder*. This is a small bladder of gas that gives the fish the *buoyancy* required at whatever depth it swims.

Fishes obtain oxygen from the water by means of *gills*. These are feathery structures behind the head which, except in the cartilaginous fishes, are covered by a flap called the *operculum*. The gills are fed with blood from the heart. In the gills, oxygen passes from the water into the blood.

Fishes feed in two ways. They either hunt and capture other fish, or large invertebrates, or they filter the minute plants and animals from the plankton through their gills. The first group of fishes have sharp teeth. The second eat and breathe at the same time.

Life of Fishes

Almost all fishes hatch from eggs, but the ways in which the parents care for them vary enormously. Many produce millions of eggs at a single spawning, leaving the eggs and newly-hatched fish unprotected. Few of these millions survive. If all did, the world's oceans would soon become full of fish. Other fishes are more involved with their young. Some sticklebacks build nests for their eggs, and the male keeps guard over the eggs and young fish. The male pipefish and the male seahorse carry the eggs in a brood pouch on the underside of the body, in which the eggs hatch. Some catfishes and mouthbreeders carry the fertilized eggs in their mouths.

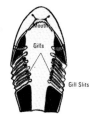

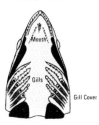

Above: Fishes breathe with their gills. The water, which contains dissolved oxygen, goes into their mouths and out through their gills. In the gills, oxygen passes into the blood and carbon dioxide passes out, into the water.

Fishes' ears are inside their bodies at the back of the skull. They have no external ears. The ears help a fish with its balance as well as with its hearing.

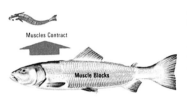

Muscles Contract

Muscle Blocks

Left: Fishes move through the water by bending their bodies in S-shaped curves. Their muscles are arranged in blocks on each side of their bodies. When one set of blocks contracts, a fish's body bends sideways.

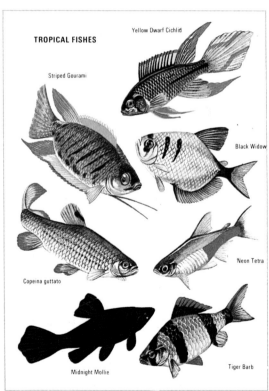

TROPICAL FISHES

Yellow Dwarf Cichlid

Striped Gourami

Black Widow

Neon Tetra

Copeina guttato

Midnight Mollie

Tiger Barb

A few fishes bear living young. These include several popular aquarium fishes such as the guppy, and some sharks. Some fishes, such as skates and dogfish, lay eggs in horny cases, popularly called 'mermaids' purses', and found on the seashore.

Ways of Life

Many fishes have strange habits fitted to their mode of life. The flying fish can glide for considerable distances over the waves, using its pectoral fins as wings. The archer fish can catch insects by squirting water at them. The mudskipper can crawl about the land and even up trees, staying alive by retaining water in its gills.

Deep-sea fishes live at depths of 600 to 6,000 metres (2,000–20,000 feet) in the ocean. At these depths, it is completely dark to the human eye, the temperature is just above freezing, and the ocean currents are very slow. The animals of this dark, cold, still world have developed strange forms and habits which enable them to survive.

Deep-sea fishes have sensitive eyes and nearly all of them produce their own light. The light organs are arranged in patterns along the body, and as each species has its own pattern, they serve as recognition signals, helping the fishes to find mates and food. Some lantern fishes have a large light organ above or below the eye which illuminates their surroundings.

Food is scarce at great depths. Plant life does not exist below a depth of about 150 metres (500 feet), where the light becomes too weak for plants to survive. Deep-sea fishes are therefore *carnivorous* animals with efficient ways of feeding. Their mouths are often gigantic, with rows of razor-sharp teeth. But the fishes themselves are rarely more than a foot long.

Some fishes produce shocks of electricity to stun their prey and to defend themselves from attacks. The shocks are produced by special muscles.

FRESHWATER FISHES

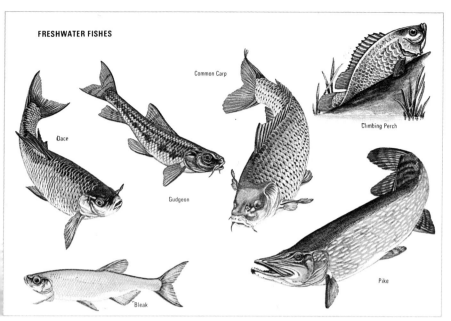

Common Carp

Dace

Gudgeon

Climbing Perch

Pike

Bleak

SALT-WATER FISHES

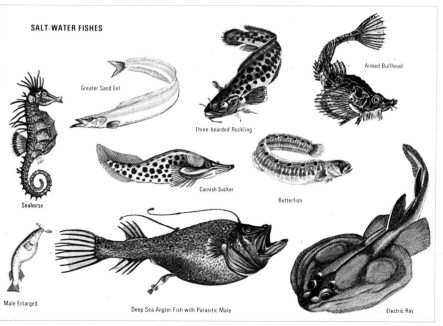

Greater Sand Eel

Armed Bullhead

Three-bearded Rockling

Seahorse

Cornish Sucker

Butterfish

Male Enlarged

Deep Sea Angler Fish with Parasitic Male

Electric Ray

Birds

Birds are the only animals that have feathers. They are warm-blooded, like human beings. They keep their bodies at a fixed high temperature whether the air is hot or cold. The feathers help to keep them warm in cold weather.

A bird's wings are specially constructed front legs, and they bear the long, sturdy feathers which are necessary for flight. Not all birds fly, however, and their wings may be poorly developed or, as in penguins, used for a completely different job: penguins use their stumpy wings for swimming.

Birds have no teeth. They rely on their beaks for catching and cutting their food, and their beaks vary according to the type of food they eat. Birds' feet also vary according to the sorts of places in which they live—ducks' feet are webbed, for example.

Because of their great mobility, birds can live almost anywhere on earth. Most birds live in trees, but many groups have taken to living wholly or partly on the ground, and others live on and around water.

Adaptations for Flight

The skeleton of a bird is well built for flight. The bones are small and thin, and therefore light, although they are strong. The long bones are hollow and are often given extra strength by criss-crossed 'struts' inside. More than half of a bird's weight is muscle, and the largest muscles are those that move the wings. These are very powerful

The wing of a bird is a modified forelimb. Here it is compared with a human arm.

Right: How birds breathe. The position of the ribs and breastbone of a bird during inspiration (left) and expiration (right) are shown by the dotted line. The respiratory movements are produced by the rib and abdominal muscles.

Below: The sequence of wing movement of a bird in flight.

muscles and must have good anchorage. This anchorage is provided by the breast-bone which has a large, thin *keel* projecting from the underside, just like the keel of a yacht. The muscles are attached to this keel. Flightless birds have only a small keel, and some of them have no keel at all.

Food and Digestion

Most birds are very active animals, and they use up a lot of energy. In order to get this energy they have to spend a great deal of time eating. Many birds, expecially the seed-eaters, have a stretchable bag near the beginning of their food canal. This bag is called the *crop*, and quite a lot of food can be swallowed and stored there. The food collected in the crop can be digested later.

Seed-eating birds and some others also have a very muscular region in the food canal which is called the *gizzard*. Seeds are ground up here, often with the aid of grit swallowed by the bird, before passing further down the canal for digestion.

The Life of a Bird

All birds reproduce by laying eggs, and they usually lay their eggs in spring or early summer. Egg-laying time is called the breeding season. The birds start by choosing their mates. Male birds often have bright colours and frequently use attractive call songs which attract mates and may also frighten other males from the chosen territory. There is a good deal of courtship and display by one or both birds, and this eventually leads to nest-building and mating. Nests are mainly places to lay eggs and rear young: they are not permanent homes. Some birds do not even bother to make a proper nest. They use a hollow in the ground or a rocky ledge.

Some birds lay as many as 20 eggs, but half a dozen is more usual. Many birds of prey lay only one or two eggs. After laying, the eggs have to be kept warm or *incubated*, and the birds do this by sitting on their eggs. Sometimes only one parent will sit on the eggs, sometimes both parents take it in turns. The eggs generally hatch in two or three weeks.

Many ground-nesting and water-nesting birds already have feathers when they hatch and they can leave the nest right away, although they still have to be looked after by their mother. Ducks and chickens are examples. Tree-living birds, however, are generally very poorly developed when they hatch, completely naked and blind and quite unable to move about. Young chicks are always very hungry, and their parents bring them a constant supply of food. Nestling birds grow and develop very rapidly as a result of the endless feeding and are ready for their first flying lesson after a few weeks.

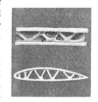

Above: The skeleton of a bird is well built for flight. The long bones are hollow and often have criss-crossed 'struts' inside. This structure, like that of a glider, saves weight without losing strength.

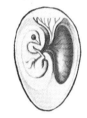

Above: A bird's egg has a rich supply of yolk for the developing embryo. The developing eggs must be kept warm and this is performed by one or both parents who incubate them while sitting on the nest.

Left: The Ostrich is the largest living bird, and lays the biggest eggs. It cannot fly but has a long neck which helps it to spot enemies. It has powerful legs and can run fast to escape quickly.

61

Amphibians

Amphibians are the class of animals that includes frogs, toads, newts, and salamanders. Many are equally at home in fresh water and on land, but almost all amphibians breed in water.

Most amphibians lay eggs that float in water or are attached to stones or water plants. The eggs hatch into larvae. A frog larva or *tadpole* has gills with which it obtains oxygen from the water to breathe. It swims by using its tail, like a fish. But as the tadpole grows, it loses its fish-like character. Lungs and limbs develop until it is able to leave the water and climb on to the land and breathe air.

Some amphibians, such as newts,

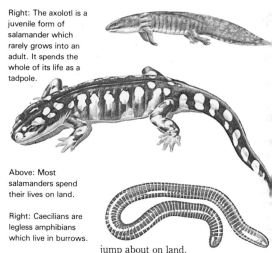

Right: The axolotl is a juvenile form of salamander which rarely grows into an adult. It spends the whole of its life as a tadpole.

Above: Most salamanders spend their lives on land.

Right: Caecilians are legless amphibians which live in burrows.

Most frogs lay their jelly-covered eggs in fresh water. The eggs hatch into tadpoles with external gills. The tadpoles grow and lose their gills. They grow legs, lose their tails, and become adult frogs.

spend most of their time in the water. Others, such as frogs and toads, are at home on land and in the water, and some, like the salamanders, live mainly on land.

Amphibians are cold-blooded animals and usually small in size, although the largest, the giant salamander of Japan, is about 2 metres long. There are three main kinds of amphibians: tailed amphibians, tail-less amphibians, and caecilians.

Tailed amphibians include the newts and salamanders. Newts live mostly in water, whereas salamanders are found mainly on land. They have long tails and four short limbs.

Tail-less amphibians include frogs and toads. They have large and powerful hind limbs with which they propel themselves through water and jump about on land.

Caecilians are legless amphibians. They live in burrows in moist soil. Some lay eggs, but others produce live young. Caecilians are found in tropical regions.

Brain   Backbone

Heart   Lungs

Intestine

Above: The body plan of an amphibian. Its skin is moist and not waterproof, and the animal breathes through it as well as through its lungs.

Below: Fowler's toad, a North American amphibian. It uses its vocal sac to make a bleating croak.

Reptiles

Reptiles are the class of animals that includes lizards and snakes, crocodiles and alligators, and turtles. Reptiles appeared on Earth about 250 million years ago. Until about 70 million years ago, some kinds of reptiles dominated the land. Some, the *dinosaurs,* grew to a great size. Others, the *pterosaurs,* flew in the air. But these creatures died out suddenly.

Reptiles are cold-blooded animals—their body temperature is the same as the temperature of their surroundings. For this reason, reptiles are not found in polar regions, where they would become too cold to survive. In regions with a cold winter, reptiles

The body plan of a typical reptile. Reptiles are vertebrate animals. They have a backbone protecting the nerve cord and a skull protecting the brain. The skin of reptiles is scaly and waterproof. They breathe through their lungs. Most reptiles have four legs, but some lizards and all the snakes are legless.

Below: The tuatara which lives on small islands off the coast of New Zealand is a 'living fossil'. It is the only living member of a group of reptiles related to the dinosaurs. The other members of this group died out millions of years ago.

Above: The caiman, a close relative of the alligator, lives in Central and South America.

hibernate. Most reptiles lay eggs, but a few bear living young.

Orders of Reptiles

There are four main groups or *orders* of living reptiles: the crocodiles and alligators; the turtles, tortoises, and terrapins; the lizards and snakes; and the tuatara.

Crocodiles and alligators make up the order *Crocodilia.* This order also includes the caimans and gavials. They are all large animals with cigar-shaped bodies and long, powerful tails. Their jaws are lined with rows of sharp teeth. They live in fresh water or salt water in tropical regions around the world, feeding on small animals.

Turtles, tortoises, and terrapins make up the order *Chelonia.* The use of

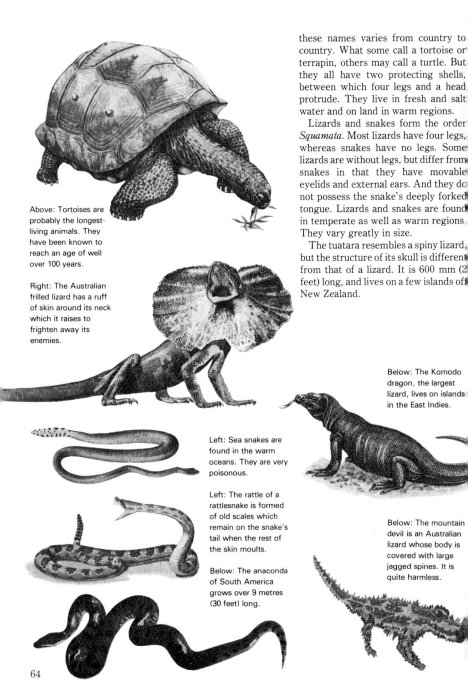

these names varies from country to country. What some call a tortoise or terrapin, others may call a turtle. But they all have two protecting shells, between which four legs and a head protrude. They live in fresh and salt water and on land in warm regions.

Lizards and snakes form the order *Squamata*. Most lizards have four legs, whereas snakes have no legs. Some lizards are without legs, but differ from snakes in that they have movable eyelids and external ears. And they do not possess the snake's deeply forked tongue. Lizards and snakes are found in temperate as well as warm regions. They vary greatly in size.

The tuatara resembles a spiny lizard, but the structure of its skull is different from that of a lizard. It is 600 mm (2 feet) long, and lives on a few islands off New Zealand.

Above: Tortoises are probably the longest-living animals. They have been known to reach an age of well over 100 years.

Right: The Australian frilled lizard has a ruff of skin around its neck which it raises to frighten away its enemies.

Below: The Komodo dragon, the largest lizard, lives on islands in the East Indies.

Left: Sea snakes are found in the warm oceans. They are very poisonous.

Left: The rattle of a rattlesnake is formed of old scales which remain on the snake's tail when the rest of the skin moults.

Below: The anaconda of South America grows over 9 metres (30 feet) long.

Below: The mountain devil is an Australian lizard whose body is covered with large jagged spines. It is quite harmless.

64

Mammals

Mammals are the dominant animals on Earth today. One of the reasons for the success of the mammals is their adaptability as a group. They are found in the icy polar seas and in the tropical rain forests. They can live in deserts and in the seas. There are flying mammals—the bats—and swimming mammals—the whales. There are also flesh-eating, fruit-eating, and grass-eating mammals.

A second reason for the success of mammals is the ability to control body temperature. They can keep warm in cold places and cool in warm places. Mammals and birds are the only animals that can do this. Others go cold when their surroundings go cold.

The Body of a Mammal

The mammals are easy to recognize, because most of them are covered by hair, fur, or wool. The fur grows from the skin, and under the skin there is a layer of muscle, and of fat. The muscles are attached to the skeleton. The mammal's skeleton is much the same as the reptile and amphibian, but is more suitable for the land.

Mammals have a skull which protects the brain, a backbone which both supports the body and protects the nerve cord, ribs which protect the heart and the lungs and help the animal to breathe, and four limbs. Most mammals' bodies are really carried on a girder—the backbone—resting on four supports—the limbs. A few, such as Man and the apes, balance on their back legs.

The mammal's body is controlled by its brain and its nervous system. The nerves run from the brain to all the parts of the body. There is a second nervous system which comes from the spinal nerve cord, and controls the movements like the beating of the heart. This continues to work when the animal is unconscious, or asleep.

Food is taken in through the mouth and digested in the stomach. It moves into the animal's intestines, where the digestion continues, and the food passes through the intestine wall into the blood stream. The blood carries the food to storage organs, such as the liver, and to the rest of the body.

Air is taken into the animal's body through the nostrils. It passes into the lungs, where the oxygen in the air is dissolved in the moisture in the lungs, and passes into the blood stream. The carbon dioxide, which is left over when the food has been used, passes out of the blood into the lungs, and is forced out of the body.

The food and the oxygen are carried round the body in the blood. The blood is pumped through the arteries—the blood vessels coming from the heart—by the heart. It is pushed along in the veins—the blood vessels going to the heart—by the blood behind it.

Below: A rabbit is a typical mammal. Its body is covered with hair, it gives birth to live young and suckles them with milk.

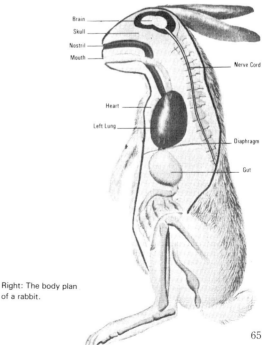

Right: The body plan of a rabbit.

Brain
Skull
Nostril
Mouth
Nerve Cord
Heart
Left Lung
Diaphragm
Gut

65

Groups of Mammals

There are three major groups of mammals. The most primitive is the monotreme group of Australia and New Guinea. These animals are the duck-billed platypus and the spiny ant-eater. They lay eggs, like reptiles, but feed their young on milk.

The second group is the marsupials, found mostly in Australia with a few in America. They keep their young in pouches. They include kangaroos, opossums, koalas, and wombats. Their young are only partly formed when they are born, and finish growing in the pouch.

The third group, the placental mammals, give birth to fully formed live young. There are 15 orders or groups of them.

Insectivora—This is a group of small animals which includes the shrews, the hedgehogs, and the moles. They are

Hedgehog

insect-eating animals, but many of them eat eggs, roots, and shoots as well as insects.

Chiroptera—This is the bat group. The bats are the only mammals that actually fly. Their arms and hands are adapted to form wings. As they fly they squeak. The echoes of the squeaks bounce back from any object so that they are warned of its presence.

Bats

Edentata—This group includes the ant-eaters, the armadillos, and the sloths. The ant-eaters have a long snout and a long, sticky tongue. This helps them to catch the ants on which

Sloth

they feed. The sloths live in trees hanging upside-down on the branches. They hang by all four feet. Sloths eat leaves.

Pholidota—This is a small group containing the pangolins, whose bodies are covered by horny scales.

Pangolin

Rodentia—The rodents include the rats, mice, gophers, and squirrels. They have four chisel-like teeth in the front of their jaws. The teeth are open-

Rat

European Lemmings

American Woodchuck

Porcupine

ended, and continue to grow throughout the rodent's life. They are constantly worn away by gnawing.

Rabbit

Lagomorpha—This group includes the rabbits and hares. They have six open-ended teeth, two more than the rodents.

Tubulidentata — This order contains only the aardvark, an African ant-eater.

Sirenia — This group consists of the seacows, manatees, and dugongs, which eat seaweed.

Hydracoidea — This small group contains the rock conies or hyraxes of Africa.

Proboscidea — This is the elephant group. The elephants are herbivores which live in Africa and southern Asia.

Cetacea — This group consists of the whales, dolphins, and porpoises. They spend all their lives in the water. Whales' bodies are completely adapted for life at sea. They are streamlined, like a fish. Their limbs are reduced to one pair of flippers. Whales are intelligent animals. They can be trained as easily as dogs.

Artiodactyla — This group includes the pigs, hippopotami, camels, deer, giraffes, yaks, sheep, cattle, goats, and antelopes.

Yak

Hippopotamus

Cow

Whale

Carnivora — These are the hunters. They include cats, dogs, bears, otters, weasels, seals, and walruses. Most of the group are flesh-eating animals.

Stoat

Leopard

Zebras at a waterhole

Perissodactyla — This group includes the horses, zebras, rhinoceroses, and tapirs. They are all herbivores.

Primates — This group includes monkeys, apes, and Man himself. Its members have eyes which face forward and mobile hands.

Tapir

Gibbons

The Living Cell

The cell is the basic unit of which all living things are made. Some of the simplest creatures, consist of just one cell. The human body is composed of millions of cells. In amoeba all the processes go on in the one cell, but in a more complicated organism there are many different kinds of cells, each designed to do a particular job.

The main difference between plant and animal cells is that the cells of plants have rigid walls of cellulose.

The basis of all cells is *protoplasm*, often called 'living jelly'. Protoplasm contains water with a complicated mixture of proteins, sugars, fatty materials, and salts. Chemical changes are going on in it all the time.

In the protoplasm are a number of fluid-filled spaces called *vacuoles*. Animal cells usually have small vacuoles, plant cells large ones. Other tiny objects in the protoplasm are rod-like *mitochondria*, believed to be concerned with releasing energy for cell activity. Plant cells normally contain *chloroplasts*, which contain chlorophyll.

The control centre of the cell is the *nucleus*. This regulates and guides the cell's activities, and carries the 'instructions' which ensure that a parrot's egg becomes a parrot, an acorn becomes an oak tree. These instructions, or *genes*, are carried on slender threads known as *chromosomes*.

Below: Diagram showing simple cell division. The nucleus divides first, and then the rest of the cell.

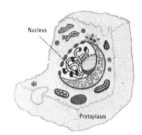

Nucleus

Protoplasm

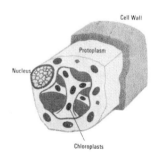

Cell Wall

Protoplasm

Nucleus

Chloroplasts

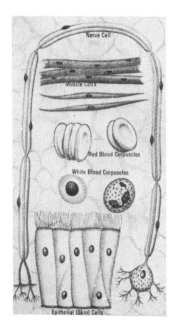

The body is built from cells just as a house is built from bricks. Different shaped cells have different jobs to do. The diagram above shows some of the cells of the human body.

The biggest difference between a plant cell and an animal cell is in the cell wall. The plant cell has a rigid cellulose cell wall. A second difference is that most plant cells have chloroplasts containing chlorophyll in them. Otherwise, plant and animal cells are similar.

The Human Body

The human body is made up of millions of tiny cells, arranged in numerous groups. Groups of similar cells which work together are called *tissues*, and different tissues are united to form *organs*.

There are five main types of tissue: *skeletal*, as in bone; *epithelium*, which provides lining and covering; *connective*, which binds organs together and packs the spaces between them; *muscle*; and *nerve*.

The study of cells, tissues, and organs is called *histology*. Anatomy is the study of the organs of the body in relation to one another.

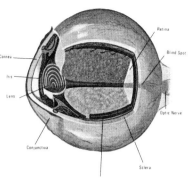

The eye is an important sense organ. It is well protected by the skull and is lubricated by the eyelid. The eye itself is covered by a tough, light-proof coat, called the sclera, with a transparent 'window'—the cornea.

Nerves

The brain and its various parts, together with the spinal cord, consist of millions of nerve cells. They may be compared to a central switch-board which receives and transmits signals. Jointly they are termed the *central nervous system*.

The brain is made up of separate grey matter (thinking) cells and white matter (pathway) cells. It controls all the conscious and unconscious thinking and movement of the body.

The central nervous system is linked to the rest of the body by the *peripheral nervous system*. The body has sense organs which enable the central nervous system to make an exact response to a given stimulus.

The skin possesses free nerve endings which respond to touch, pain, and temperature.

The eyes have light-sensitive cells which transmit signals to the brain by way of the *optic* nerve.

The ear is the body's organ of hearing. It receives sound waves which are transmitted as signals along the *auditory* nerve to the brain. The ear also possesses a mechanism which controls the body's sense of balance.

The *olfactory* cells provide the body with its sense of smell. These *chemoreceptors* (sense organs dealing with chemicals) are embedded in the epithelial lining of the nose. The tongue also possesses chemoreceptors in the form of *taste-buds*.

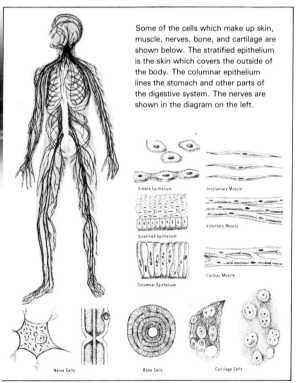

Some of the cells which make up skin, muscle, nerves, bone, and cartilage are shown below. The stratified epithelium is the skin which covers the outside of the body. The columnar epithelium lines the stomach and other parts of the digestive system. The nerves are shown in the diagram on the left.

Simple Epithelium

Stratified Epithelium

Columnar Epithelium

Involuntary Muscle

Voluntary Muscle

Cardiac Muscle

Nerve Cells

Bone Cells

Cartilage Cells

Vertebrae

Spinal Cord

Bone and Cartilage
The human body is supported by a skeleton of hard bones. These carry the full weight of the body, and help to protect the body's delicate and sensitive organs.

A bone consists of layers of hard calcium phosphate and other materials. It has a rich blood supply, and spaces in it are filled with a fatty marrow in which red blood corpuscles are produced.

Cartilage is also a skeletal tissue. It acts as a shock absorber for the body. It is tough and very strong, resists compression and extension, and yet is slightly elastic.

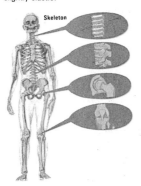

Skeleton

Skin
Skin, the outer covering of the body, consists of a sheet of epithetal cells cemented together. Skin acts as a protective coat for underlying muscles. Evaporation of water (perspiration) from the sweat glands cools the body when it gets hot.

Section of Skin

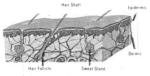

Hair Shaft   Epidermis

Dermis

Hair Follicle   Sweat Gland

Muscle
Three kinds of muscles provide all the body movements. *Involuntary*, or *unstriped*, muscles include those over which we generally have no conscious control. These are found, for example, in the walls of the intestine and blood vessels, and the pupil of the eye. *Voluntary*, or *striped*, muscles include those which we can consciously control. Muscles of the limbs, neck, and abdomen are of this type, which accounts for the largest number of muscles in the body.

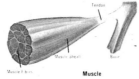

Tendon

Muscle Sheath   Bone

Muscle Fibres

Muscle

Digestion and Absorption
The human body needs food to live. The foods we eat are made up of sugary and starchy carbohydrates, fats, proteins, minerals, vitamins, and water. The body digests (breaks down) these foods to provide energy and body building materials.

Food enters the body through the mouth, where the teeth grind it into smaller particles. This allows the first digestive juice in saliva to act.

After the food is swallowed it passes down a thick tube (*oesophagus*) to the stomach. There it is sterilized by hydrochloric acid, and attacked by more digestive juices which start the breakdown of proteins. Small quantities of digested food are absorbed through the stomach lining and the remainder travels into a long, narrow tube, the *small intestine*.

In the small intestine, various glands produce secretions to continue the digestive process. The liver produces bile salts which split up large fat droplets into smaller ones. The pancreas releases its alkaline juice which contains substances (*enzymes*) able to break down proteins to smaller units, starch to maltose, and fats to fatty acids and glycerol. The first loop of the small intestine (*duodenum*) contains glands in its walls that also produce an alkaline digestive juice.

When the food has been broken down completely, it is absorbed through the thin walls of the small intestine. Amino-acids (from proteins) and glucose pass into a network of tiny blood vessels which then join up and carry the food to the liver. The fatty acids and glycerol, obtained from fatty foods, reach the liver by an indirect route through the lymph vessels and the heart. The *liver* acts rather like a warehouse, holding back much of the digested food and releasing it gradually as the body needs it.

When all the food materials have been absorbed, the small intestine is left with a watery residue containing indigestible material. This residue passes to the *large intestine* which is concerned mainly with the absorption of water. When most of the water has been taken back into the body, the residue is passed out as *faeces*.

Digestive Tract

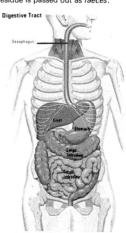

Oesophagus

Liver

Stomach

Large Intestine

Small Intestine

Excretion
The removal of waste products from the body (excretion) is the main function of the kidneys. Blood passes through the kidneys, which filter out excess water and waste materials such

Kidney   Renal Artery   Renal Vein

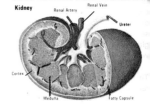

Ureter

Cortex

Medulla   Fatty Capsule

as ammonia and urea. This filtered material, urine, is carried from the kidneys in two tubes (*ureters*) which take it to the bladder. From there it passes to the outside through a tube called the *urethra*.

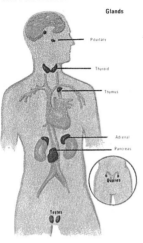

Glands

Glands

Glands produce chemical substances. There are two main types: *exocrine* glands which release their secretions for local action into a duct (e.g. the sweat glands, salivary glands, liver, and pancreas); and *endocrine*, or *ductless*, glands which release their fluids directly into the blood stream to affect a distant part or the body as a whole (e.g. the pituitary, adrenals, thyroid, and parathyroid). The pancreas has both endocrine and exocrine regions.

The *pituitary*, suspended from the underside of the brain, is called the master gland. It weighs only one-sixth of an ounce, yet it has a great effect upon the whole body. The hormones it secretes affect: growth and the building up and breaking down processes of the body (*metabolism*); water and salt loss through the kidneys; the sex glands; the thyroid and adrenal glands; and the smooth muscle in the walls of blood vessels.

The *thyroid* gland secretes *thyroxin*. This hormone causes an increase in the rate of chemical reactions within cells.

The *pancreas* produces the hormone

insulin which regulates the blood sugar level and controls the rate at which glucose is released from the liver.

Adrenal glands secrete adrenalin which increases the heartbeat and prepares a frightened person for action.

Male and female bodies possess glands for reproduction. The female reproductive organs consist of almond-shaped ovaries which produce unfertilized eggs (*ova*) at regular intervals. Male glands of reproduction are the testes which produce millions of spermatozoa (sperm).

The Blood System

The blood acts as the body's transport system, connecting up the various parts of the body and carrying oxygen and food cells. Waste products of metabolism are also carried by the blood to the kidneys for elimination from the body. The blood also helps to keep the body at an even temperature, and it helps to fight invading germs.

The body contains about 5 litres (9 pints) of blood which is driven at a high pressure to the tissues. The fluid part (*plasma*) contains the food supply needed by the body cells. In the plasma float millions of red and white blood corpuscles.

The red corpuscles, manufactured in bone marrow, contain a pigment (*haemoglobin*) which carries oxygen from the lungs to the tissues where it is released. Carbon dioxide, formed when food is used up in the body, dissolves in the blood plasma and is carried back to the lungs where it escapes into the air.

The white corpuscles in blood help to combat disease by destroying bacteria. Substances produced by bacteria may also kill white blood cells.

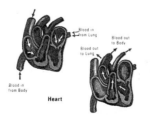

Heart

The blood is pumped around the body by the heart. The human heart is a muscular, four-chambered 'bag' situ-

ated in the chest cavity between the lungs. The two upper chambers are called *auricles* and the two lower ones are called *ventricles*.

The blood vessels carrying blood away from the heart are called *arteries*. They branch to all parts of the body and, as they get further from the heart, they get smaller and smaller until they become minute *capillaries*. These capillaries spread through all the tissues, giving up food and oxygen, and then they join up again to form *veins* which carry the blood back to the heart.

Respiration

The energy the body needs for growth and movement is obtained by the 'burning' (*oxidation*) of food materials within the body tissues. The oxygen essential for this process is found in air. It is absorbed into the blood stream in the lungs. At the same time, the blood gives up the waste carbon dioxide it has brought from the tissues.

The lungs are situated in a cavity sur-

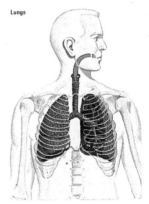

Lungs

rounded below by a muscular upward-domed sheet (*diaphragm*) and on all other sides by the ribs.

During the inhaling of air (*inspiration*), the diaphragm muscles contract, so flattening the sheet, and the ribs are pulled out by muscles to enlarge the lung cavity. When exhaling (*expiration*), the muscles relax, the lung cavity becomes smaller, and air is forced out of the lungs.

71

The Plant Kingdom

Most plants are fixed to one spot, and consist of roots, stems, and leaves.

Living things are divided into two main groups—plants and animals. Most plants are fixed to one spot, but the majority of animals can move from place to place. Plants go on growing throughout their lives, whereas animals stop growing when they reach a certain point. But the most important difference between plants and animals is in the way they get their food. Plants can make food from simple materials in the air and the soil. Animals cannot do this; they have to obtain ready-made food from plants or from other animals that have eaten plants.

Photosynthesis

The food-making process of plants is called *photosynthesis*, which means 'making by light', because it uses the energy of light. Most of the energy comes from sunlight, and photosynthesis normally takes place only in the daytime.

Light falling on the plant is trapped by the green pigment called *chlorophyll*, which is found mainly in the leaves. The leaves of a plant are therefore arranged so that they receive as much light as possible—no leaf completely overshadows another, and there are no wasteful gaps between the leaves. In this way, the plant makes the best possible use of the sunlight.

The raw materials used in photosynthesis are water and carbon dioxide gas. Water is obtained from the soil and carbon dioxide is obtained from the air. Inside the plant, the light energy trapped by the chlorophyll is used in a complicated series of reactions. The end result is that the water and carbon dioxide are joined together to form glucose sugar. Oxygen is given off during the process and returned to the air.

The glucose sugar provides the plant with energy for growth, but the plant cannot build new parts from sugar alone. It must also have minerals, such as nitrates and potash, which it obtains from the soil. These are combined with sugar to form proteins, the basis of all living material. The proteins are used to build new material.

The Carbon Cycle

The amount of carbon dioxide in the atmosphere stays constant at about 0.03%. Huge quantities of carbon dioxide are removed every day by plants and yet the total remains the same. How can this be? The answer is that carbon dioxide is being returned to the air all the time. When animals breathe, they take in oxygen (which is given out by plants) and give off carbon dioxide.

This whole system of carbon dioxide being taken from the air by plants and then returned by various routes is called the *carbon cycle*. It is vital to all living things because if the carbon dioxide were not returned the plants would soon exhaust the supply.

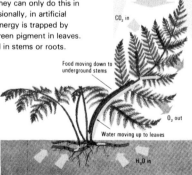

The biggest difference between plants and animals is that plants can make their own food while animals cannot. Plants make their food from carbon dioxide in the air and from the water and nutrient salts in the soil. They can only do this in sunlight, or, occasionally, in artificial light. The Sun's energy is trapped by chlorophyll, the green pigment in leaves. The food is stored in stems or roots.

Algae

The simplest members of the plant kingdom are the *algae*. These are flowerless plants which include all the seaweeds and the tiny floating plants called plankton. They range from microscopic cells and threads to huge seaweeds. Many of the smaller algae live in ponds and streams, and they often form a thick green scum on the surface. Some seaweeds are brown or red, but they still contain chlorophyll and make food in the normal way.

Fungi

Moulds and toadstools belong to a group called *fungi*. These plants have no chlorophyll, and have to get food from other organisms. Most fungi live in the soil and get food from dead leaves. Some grow on living plants.

Fungi have no flowers or seeds and they reproduce by scattering clouds of dust-like spores.

Mosses and Liverworts

The *mosses* and *liverworts* are all small green plants, living mainly in damp and shady places. Most of them have stems and leaves, but there are no real roots. These plants usually form 'mats' or 'cushions' on the ground. There are no flowers or seeds and the plants scatter tiny spores.

Ferns

Ferns are generally much larger than mosses and they are more complex in structure. They have real roots, and the leaves are usually divided into numerous leaflets. Like the mosses, the ferns have no flowers or seeds. They produce clouds of spores, usually in little brown patches under the leaves.

Conifers

The *conifers*, such as pines and larches, do not have real flowers, but do produce seeds. The seeds are carried in woody cones. Conifers are usually evergreens, and they have needle-like leaves.

Flowering Plants

The great majority of plants we see are *flowering plants*. The bright, scented flowers attract insects, which pollinate the flowers and ensure the seeds develop. Some flowering plants scatter pollen for the wind to carry. Grasses are among the best examples. Flowering plants protect their seeds inside fruits, such as pods or berries.

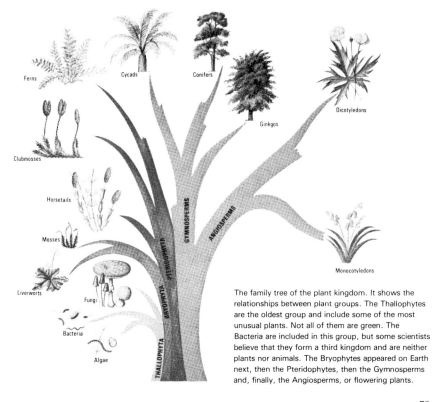

The family tree of the plant kingdom. It shows the relationships between plant groups. The Thallophytes are the oldest group and include some of the most unusual plants. Not all of them are green. The Bacteria are included in this group, but some scientists believe that they form a third kingdom and are neither plants nor animals. The Bryophytes appeared on Earth next, then the Pteridophytes, then the Gymnosperms and, finally, the Angiosperms, or flowering plants.

73

Flowering Plants

Flowering plants belong to one of two great classes, *monocotyledons* or *dicotyledons*, according to whether their seeds possess one or two cotyledons (seed leaves) respectively. There are other differences too. Monocotyledons are almost all herbs (non-woody plants), they have leaves with parallel veins, stem-veins scattered throughout the stem, and flower-parts (stamens, carpels, petals, and sepals) in threes or multiples of three. Dicotyledons contain many woody species. Their leaves are generally net-veined, and the stem veins occur in a definite cylinder down the stem. Their flower parts are generally found in fours and fives.

The life of a flowering plant begins at the moment of fertilization, that is when a male cell from a pollen grain joins with a tiny egg cell in a flower. The fertilized cell eventually grows and forms a new plant. But the newly fertilized cell cannot grow without food, and this food must be provided by the parent plant. So the little cell remains inside the ovary of the parent plant. There it grows and forms a little embryo. The embryo, with its surrounding food reserves and its tough coat, is called a seed. It is ready to begin life on its own.

Germination

Protected by the tough coats, seeds can usually remain at rest for quite a long time. They will not grow unless they have both water and warmth. But when conditions are right they spring to life and germinate. The germinating seed absorbs water and swells up. The seed coat bursts and the little root pushes its way out, soon followed by the shoot, which produces the stem and leaves. The young plant soon begins to make its own food by photosynthesis.

Flowers and Pollination

The main function of the flower is to

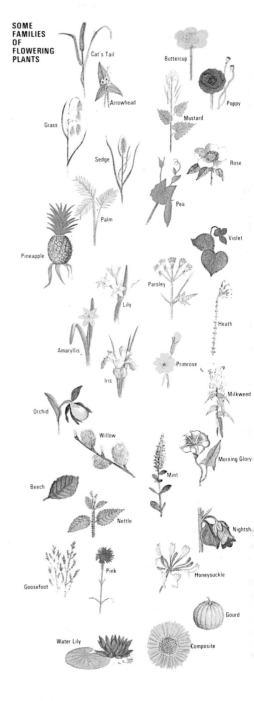

Cat's Tail
Buttercup
Arrowhead
Poppy
Mustard
Grass
Sedge
Rose
Pea
Palm
Violet
Pineapple
Parsley
Lily
Heath
Amaryllis
Primrose
Iris
Milkweed
Orchid
Willow
Morning Glory
Beech
Mint
Nettle
Nightsh
Pink
Honeysuckle
Goosefoot
Gourd
Water Lily
Composite

reproduce the plant by forming more seeds, and the essential parts of the flower are the *stamens* and the *carpels*. The stamens produce the pollen, while the carpels contain one or more ovules which later become seeds. Most flowers contain both stamens and carpels, but some plants carry their stamens and carpels in separate flowers. The vegetable marrow is a good example. Some species even carry their stamens and carpels on different plants. The holly does this.

As well as the stamens and carpels, most flowers have *sepals* and *petals*. The sepals are on the outside and their main job is to protect the young flower before it opens. They fold back or fall off when the flower opens. The petals are generally brightly coloured and their main function is to attract insects to the flowers. They are aided in this job by the flower's scent and nectar. The insects are very important for the flowers because they carry pollen about with them and some of it rubs off on to the carpels. This transfer of pollen from the stamens to the carpels is called *pollination*.

Although most flowers are pollinated by insects, the grasses and a good many trees are pollinated by the wind. They have dull-coloured flowers.

Fruits and Seeds

When a pollen grain has landed on a stigma of the right kind of flower it sends out a tiny tube which grows down into the carpel. Cells from the pollen grain move down the tube and one of them joins with an egg cell inside one of the ovules to begin seed formation as already described.

While the seed and embryo are developing in the ovule, the surrounding carpel is also changing. It becomes the fruit. There are many kinds of fruits, ranging from hard nuts to soft berries. The job of the fruit is to protect the developing seed or seeds and help scatter them when ripe.

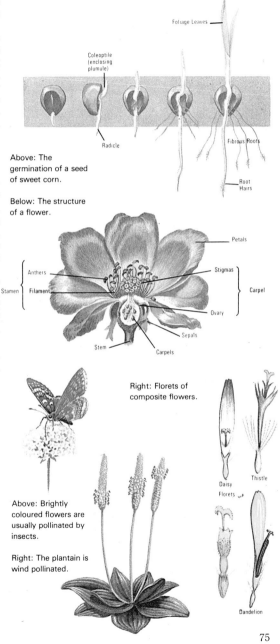

Above: The germination of a seed of sweet corn.

Below: The structure of a flower.

Right: Florets of composite flowers.

Above: Brightly coloured flowers are usually pollinated by insects.

Right: The plantain is wind pollinated.

75

Trees

A tree is a large plant with a thick, woody stem called a trunk. Apart from this, however, trees are not really any different from the other plants we see around us in fields and gardens. They all start life as seeds, they all carry leaves, and most of them eventually bear flowers. Shrubs or bushes are similar to trees but, instead of having a central trunk, they have several main stems all more or less the same size and all coming from about ground level.

Each kind of tree has its own pattern of branching and, although no two trees are exactly alike, it is possible to recognize some kinds of trees by their shape alone.

Wood and Bark

Like all plants, trees make food in their leaves. They need plenty of water for this and the trunk of the tree consists mainly of water-carrying tubes. These are packed densely together and, being

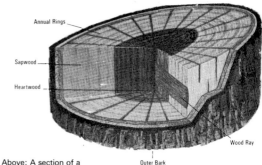
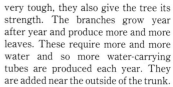

Above: A section of a tree-trunk with a wedge cut from it. The dark wood in the middle is the heartwood. The paler wood is the sapwood. The wood rays are living cells through the trunk of the tree.

Below: The largest group of trees is the Flowering Tree group. They have broad leaves and branching leaf veins.

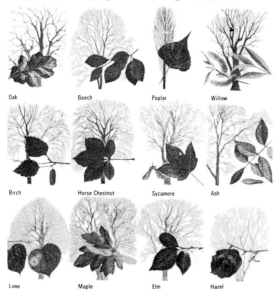

Oak   Beech   Poplar   Willow

Birch   Horse Chestnut   Sycamore   Ash

Lime   Maple   Elm   Hazel

very tough, they also give the tree its strength. The branches grow year after year and produce more and more leaves. These require more and more water and so more water-carrying tubes are produced each year. They are added near the outside of the trunk.

As autumn approaches and growth slows down, the size of the new tubes gets smaller and then production stops altogether. When spring returns and the sap starts to flow again tube production re-starts. These spring-formed tubes are much larger than the autumn-formed tubes and, if the tree is cut down, one can see distinct lines between the autumn and spring wood. These are called annual rings and, by counting them, one can find out the age of the tree.

The earliest water-carrying tubes gradually get squashed in the centre of the trunk and they are then unable to carry water. They form a very dense wood called *heartwood*. Wood which is still carrying water is called *sapwood*.

Around the outside of the trunk there is a layer of bark. It consists largely of cork and it is often quite soft. Its job is to protect the wood underneath. New layers of cork are produced each year as the trunk gets thicker, and the older bark on the outside splits and perhaps flakes off. The cork oak, which comes from the Mediterranean area, produces extra thick cork which can be stripped off every few years

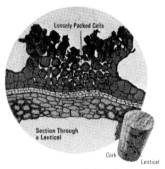

Air enters the tree-trunk through lenticels—groups of loosely packed cells in the bark. It is the lenticels in a bottle cork that allow the air through.

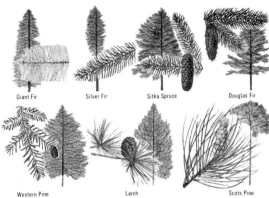

Giant Fir   Silver Fir   Sitka Spruce   Douglas Fir

Western Pine   Larch   Scots Pine

Above: The conifers have narrow leaves. Below: Little remains of the thick forests which once covered Britain.

without hurting the tree. This is where we get bottle corks and other cork objects from.

Conifers

There are two main groups of trees: those with cones (the conifers), and those with flowers. The conifers include pine, larch, spruce (used for Christmas trees), cedar, and yew. Conifers have narrow, needle-like leaves and most of them are evergreens. This means that they carry leaves all through the year, although each leaf lives only two or three years. Coniferous trees have no flowers and they generally carry their seeds in woody cones.

The tough leaves of conifers are able to stand up to strong winds and severe cold, and so we find that conifers are the dominant trees in the cooler parts of the world.

Flowering Trees

The flowering trees generally have broad, flat leaves and many kinds of trees can be recognized from their leaves alone. The trees that grow in tropical forests are usually *evergreens*—because conditions allow them to grow all the year round—but most of those growing in the temperate regions are *deciduous* trees, which drop all their

Prehistoric Britain
Britain today

leaves in autumn and stand bare through the winter. The next year's leaves are wrapped up in the winter buds which can be used to identify the trees. Deciduous trees include elm, beech, maple, ash, and oak.

Horse chestnut, lilac, apple, and many other garden trees possess large and attractive flowers. These flowers attract insects, which feed on the nectar and then carry pollen to the next flower they visit. This transfer of pollen from flower to flower is called pollination and it is very important because the trees cannot form seeds without it. But not all trees have bright, showy flowers. Many tree flowers are dull green and very hard to see. Because they do not see the flowers, many people do not realize that trees such as oaks and elms have flowers. But they do: the oak carries little strings of greenish flowers, like the catkins of hazel. These dull flowers are not visited by insects and they simply scatter their pollen in the wind.

Tree Products

Wood has always been a very important material to man, first of all for making his spears and arrows and for building his fires, and later for building his houses. Even today timber is still a most important building material.

The other major commodity that we get from trees is food, usually as fruit.

77

Peoples of the World

Human beings all belong to the same species. But varying geographical conditions and climates have resulted in the *evolution* (development by change) of different groups called races.

It is believed that all people originally came from one common ancestral type, but the various groups now have distinct and characteristic differences. Some are tall, fair-skinned, and blue-eyed, often with light-coloured wavy hair; and others are very dark-skinned, or black, and have short woolly hair, and deep brown eyes. Some, again, are small and slimly built, with long straight black hair, and slanting almond-shaped eyes. But because people move about and intermarry, most countries have a mixture of types.

Caucasoid People: An Arab of Egypt (left), a woman of Bulgaria (centre), and a woman of India (right).

having a rounder head, and is shorter on the whole, and often has brown eyes. This type is found chiefly in central Europe and in a broad belt of land stretching from western France as far as Persia in the east. Around the Mediterranean, people are dark-haired, but inclined to be short, and slightly built. Caucasoid people are also found in northern Africa and the

Races of Man

In Europe, most people are of the Caucasoid race, but are a mixture of several types within it. The Nordic types are found mainly in the north and west, and as a rule these people have long narrow heads, fair colouring, and blue eyes, and are quite tall. The Alpine type is darker than the Nordic,

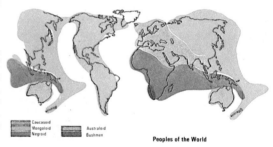

Caucasoid
Mongoloid
Negroid
Australoid
Bushmen

Peoples of the World

Above: A map of the world showing the distribution of various races before recent migration.

Mongoloid People: Two women of Japan (left), a man of Hong Kong (centre), and an Indian farmer of Peru (right).

Middle East, and in places such as North America.

Mongoloid races are found all across the continent of Asia, and have spread east, through migrations, to become the Eskimos and American Indians; south-east into the Pacific Islands; and west to become the Lapps of Europe. Their heads are round, covered in long straight hair, and their skins are yellow or brown. As a rule, they have short flat noses and slanting eyes.

In Africa south of the Sahara the people are of the Negroid type (short woolly hair, black skin and eyes). Farther south still, the Congo pygmies, Bushmen, and Hottentots of southern Africa differ greatly and are thought to be of different races.

Both North and South America are believed to have been peopled originally by very early migrations from eastern Asia. The many tribes of American Indians are descended from these early migrants. White Americans are descended from Europeans.

The Australian aborigine is of the Australoid type, with dark skin, wavy hair, and overhanging eyebrows. Similar types are found in India.

Negroid People: A warrior and his wife of New Guinea (right), and an African Negro (below).

Two aborigines of Australia (left), a group of Maoris of New Zealand (right), and a group of pygmies of Congo (below).

Population

The world population is at present reckoned to be over 4,400 million. It is still rising rapidly, especially in Africa and Latin America, and may well reach over 6,200 million by the end of the present century. Advances in medical knowledge, improved sanitation, and superior technical developments have all contributed to a rapid increase in population.

Most of the world's people are concentrated on a fraction of the Earth's surface, in those parts where soil and climate make it comparatively easy to live. The most densely massed populations are found in Western Europe, the United States, the Nile Valley, India, Java, China, and Japan.

79

Literature

Literature is a broad term which covers almost any composition which has a permanent record in writing or in print. It includes poems, ballads, stories, novels, plays, essays, philosophical writings, history, and biographies of people. The term is usually used to describe works which have a lasting interest and value.

The earliest books were long scrolls of parchment or papyrus, rolled on to two sticks, or incised clay tablets baked in the sun. The modern book, of folded sheets which can be sewn together, is called a codex, and it came into use about A.D. 300. Books were rare and valuable because they were all written by hand. The invention of printing in the mid-1400s made it possible to produce many copies of a book quickly and cheaply.

Some of the earliest forms of literature were narrative poems. Many of these poems were histories of various peoples, or of the legends which they had invented to explain their origins, and of their heroes, both real and fictional. Famous examples are the

Above: An ancient bust of the poet Homer.

Right: A Mystery play being performed on a cart at Coventry in the Middle Ages. Such plays helped to teach religion to people who could not read.

Left: Part of *The Prologue* from an early illuminated edition of Chaucer's *Canterbury Tales*. It is a fine example of a handwritten book.

sagas of Iceland, and the epic poems of ancient Greece which are attributed to the blind poet Homer. Epic poems of this kind were usually added to over many years.

Greek and Roman writers produced what we call *classical* plays, both tragedies and comedies, written to be performed in open-air theatres. After the collapse of the Roman Empire in A.D. 476 the drama declined, until it was revived by the medieval Christian Church in the form of mystery plays. These plays were designed to teach

religious truths. In time, the theatre became less religious, and many great plays were written to be acted. They have been printed in book form, and are an important part of literature.

Apart from plays—by such writers as William Shakespeare in English and Molière in French—most literature was for many years factual rather than fiction. Stories were still often written in verse, as for example the *Canterbury Tales* of Geoffrey Chaucer. Towards the middle of the 17th century, however, many romances were written, and novels began to appear. In time the novel became one of the most popular forms of literature.

Languages

There are about 2,800 different languages, not including *dialects* (local variations). The language spoken by the greatest number of people is Chinese, with about 600 million speakers. English comes next, with 400 million, then Hindi (over 200 million), and Spanish (about 150 million).

Some languages die as people stop using them. Sanskrit and Latin are now dead languages. But many words in living languages come from Latin and Sanskrit words. All languages change gradually. People invent new words and new words come into the language from other languages.

There are several families of languages. The largest is the *Indo-European* family, spoken by half the world's people. This family contains eight branches: the *Germanic* branch, with German, English, Dutch, and the Scandinavian languages; the *Romance* branch, with French, Italian, and Spanish; the *Balto-Slavic* branch, with Russian; and the *Indo-Iranian, Greek, Celtic, Armenian,* and *Albanian*

branches. The only other large family is the *Sino-Tibetan* family, spoken by a quarter of the world's population. Chinese is a Sino-Tibetan language.

Languages are written down in alphabets—groups of characters or symbols. English is written in the *Roman* alphabet with 26 letters. Most other European languages are written in this alphabet, but the actual characters or letters may be pronounced in different ways.

There are several other alphabets in common use. The *Greek* alphabet has 24 letters. It is used only in Greece, although scientists use the letters as symbols in their work. The word 'alphabet' comes from its first two letters: (alpha) and (beta). Russians and other Slavs use the *Cyrillic* alphabet, which developed from Greek about 1,100 years ago.

Above: The ancient Egyptians used picture signs, or hieroglyphics.

Left: The Rosetta Stone was written in the three scripts of Egypt — hieroglyphics, demotic, and Greek.

Right: Characters of five different alphabets (left to right), Arabic, Hebrew, Greek, Cyrillic, and Roman.

Arabic	Hebrew	Greek	Cyrillic	Roman
١	א	α	a	A
ب	כ	β	б	B
ج، چ	כ، ב	κ, σ	к, с	C
د	ד	δ	д	D
ه	ה	ε, η	е, э	E
ف	ם	φ	ф, ө	F
ج	ג	γ	г	G
ه	ה	'	г	H
ى	'	ι	и, й	I
ج	—	—	дж	J
ك	כ	κ	к	K
ل	ל	λ	л	L
م	מ	μ	м	M
ن	נ	ν	н	N
و	٩	ο, ω	о	O
پ	פ	π	п	P
ق	ק	ϙ	—	Q
ر	ר	ρ	р	R
س، ص	שׁ، ס	σ, ς	с	S
ط	ת، ט	τ	т	T
و	'	υ	и, ю	U
و	'	υ	в	V
و	'	ƒ	—	V V
—	—	ξ	кс	X
خ	،	ι, υ	я	Y
ز، ظ	צ، ז	ζ	з	Z

81

Great Religions

There have been many religions in the history of the world. From the earliest times people have believed in and worshipped a god, or more than one god. Primitive man worshipped simple things, such as stones, the Sun, or a river. But since that time men have evolved many different faiths. These are some of the most widespread and influential religions today.

Christianity

Christianity is the religion of those who follow the teaching and example of Jesus Christ. Jesus preached a doctrine of universal love and brotherhood. His teachings and the story of his life are related in the New Testament. Despite the simplicity of Christ's doctrines, the religion has been complicated by the many interpretations put upon them. Today there are about 1,000 million Christians.

Islam

In all there are about 500 million Muslims. Muslims are followers of Mohammed (A.D. 570–632), whom they regard as the last great prophet and messenger of Allah (God). The sacred book of Islam is the Koran. All good Muslims must observe the 'five pillars' of their faith—the first is confession of faith in one God and Mohammed. The second is prayer, five times a day. The third is almsgiving. The fourth is fasting. And the fifth is pilgrimage to Mecca, the birthplace of Mohammed.

Hinduism

More than four-fifths (about 500 million) of the people of India are Hindus. Hinduism is both religion and a way of life. Union with Brahma, the supreme, all-embracing spirit, is the goal of the Hindu. He can achieve this by practising *yoga* and self-discipline.

Above: Icons, depicting sacred subjects such as the madonna and child, were often regarded as sacred in the Eastern Orthodox Church. Right: An archbishop is one of the spiritual leaders of the Church of England.

Above: Hindus regard the River Ganges as sacred. Hindu pilgrims bathe in it and drink the water.

Right: In Japan, Shinto families often worship at their private 'temples' where, they believe, the spirits of their ancestors are enshrined.

Below: A young Muslim kneels and prays to Allah.

If a man fails to achieve this union he is reborn, either to a higher or lower form of life, depending upon the way he has led his former life.

Confucianism

Confucianism is not really a religion but a philosophy. Confucius was an ancient Chinese scholar. The basis of his teaching was the Golden Rule: 'Do not do unto others as you would not have others do unto you.' There are over 300 million Confucianists.

Buddhism

Buddhism is the religion of about 200 million people. Buddhists do not worship a god, but seek to attain the state of *nirvana* (enlightenment) in which there is no desire, no suffering, and no existence as we know it. According to Siddhartha Gautama (the Buddha who founded the religion), the way to this state is by the 'noble eightfold path' whose steps comprise a code of conduct covering all aspects of a man's life. Like Hindus, Buddhists believe that all creatures are born many times.

Judaism

Judaism is based on the teachings of the Old Testament and the Talmud. Many of its beliefs concerning God and morals are shared by the Christians. Jews believe that they are God's chosen people and that one day a Messiah will come to establish God's kingdom on earth. There are 15 million Jews.

Other Important Faiths

Jainism and **Sikhism** are two widespread Indian sects which practise much modified forms of Hinduism.
Shintoism is a Japanese religion based on nature and ancestor worship.
Taoism is a mystical Eastern religion which preaches a creed of compassion, humility and non-violence.
Zoroastrianism is an ancient Persian religion whose creed is based on the fight between good and evil in man.

Right: The sound of the Ram's Horn ushers in the Jewish New Year (Rosh Hashanah) and the start of ten days of penitence.

Below: Statues of the Buddha or Enlightened One, who founded the religion, play a great part in the devotions of Buddhists.

Architecture

In prehistoric days, man was a hunter. He wandered from place to place in search of food, resting when he could. The story of architecture and buildings begins when he settled in one place to grow crops and tend cattle. Only then did man begin to build.

As far back as 3500 B.C., however, long before people in northern Europe had left their caves, a kingdom existed in Egypt. Out of this kingdom grew the temples, the tombs, and statues of Ancient Egypt.

The Greeks brought architecture to Europe. Their simple and balanced methods of building have become known as the *Classical* style. From about 700 B.C., this style had a great influence on architecture in Europe. The Greek design of the columns which supported buildings became known as the *Doric, Ionic,* and *Corinthian Orders.*

Later, the Romans went ahead of the Greeks with their use of the arch and the vault. A vault is a roof that is supported by a number of arches.

Medieval and Modern

In the 10th to 12th centuries *Romanesque* was the main style of architecture in Europe. 'Romanesque' literally means 'the style of the Romans'. At first this was simple and sturdy, but buildings became larger and more elaborate as time went on. Next came the *Gothic* style, with its lighter and more graceful buildings.

Then, in Italy in the 15th century, there was a revival of the Classical style in art and architecture. This was the beginning of the *Renaissance* period, which literally means 'rebirth'. It lasted until about the 19th century, when there was a return to a kind of Gothic and Romanesque style, based on modern structural inventions. Today architecture is more functional.

Above: St. Paul's Cathedral, London.

Right: Part of the UNESCO building in Paris, an example of modernistic design.

Below: The Doric, Ionic, and Corinthian orders of architecture. The Tuscan order is a simplified form of Doric.

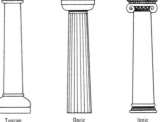

Tuscan   Doric   Ionic   Corinthian

GLOSSARY OF ARCHITECTURAL TERMS

Abacus A slab forming the upper part of a column capital.

Alcove A recess in the wall of a room.

Apse A vaulted semicircular or polygonal (many-sided) termination, usually to a chancel or chapel.

Arcade A row of arches.

Baluster A short post or column.

Balustrade A row of balusters.

Boss An ornamental knob or projection covering the intersection of ribs of a vault.

Canopy A small sculptured covering over a statue, tomb, altar, etc.

Clerestory The upper part of the main walls of a church, pierced by windows.

Corbel A block of stone projecting from a wall to support a beam.

Crypt An underground chamber usually below the east end of a church.

Dormer Window A window placed vertically in a sloping roof.

Facade The front of a building.

Facing The finish applied to the outer surface of a building.

Gable The triangular upper portion of a wall to carry a sloping roof.

Grille An openwork screen.

Jamb The straight side of an archway, doorway, or window.

Mezzanine A low intermediate storey between ground floor and first storey.

Mosaic Ornamental surface of small cubes of coloured stone, glass, marble, or tile embedded in cement.

Piazza An open space surrounded by buildings.

Relief Carving or modelling in which the forms stand out from a flat surface.

Rib A projecting band on a ceiling or vault.

Rotunda A building or room that is circular in plan and usually domed.

Shaft The trunk of a column between the base and the capital.

Stucco Plasterwork.

Transom A horizontal bar of stone or wood in a window.

Wainscot The timber lining to walls.

Egyptian: Temple of Amenhotep III (Luxor)

Byzantine: Santa Sophia, Constantinople

Romanesque: Pisa Cathedral

Italian Gothic: Milan Cathedral

Baroque: Santiago de Compostela

Greek Doric: Temple of Neptune, Paestum

Roman: Arch of Constantine, Rome

French Late Gothic: St. Ouen, Rouen

English Decorated: York Minster

Roman Renaissance: St. Peter's, Rome

Anglo-Classic: St. Paul's Cathedral

Modern: Empire State Building, New York

DEVELOPMENT OF ARCHITECTURE

B.C.

3200 Egyptian Period begins. Great Pyramid.

1800 Stonehenge begun.

700 Greek Doric.

400 Greek Ionic and Corinthian.

147 Roman Period begins.

A.D.

300 Byzantine Period begins (Eastern Roman Empire).

800 Crowning of Charlemagne. Romanesque Period begins (in northern Europe).

1066 Norman Period begins (in England).

1140 Gothic Period begins (in France).

1175 Early English Period begins.

1200 High Gothic Period begins (in France).

1245 Building starts on Westminster Abbey.

1299 Decorated Period begins (in England).

1330 Perpendicular Period begins (in England).

1400 Early Renaissance Period begins (in Italy).

1485 Tudor Period begins.

1500 High Renaissance Period begins (in Italy: Michelangelo).

1530 French Renaissance Period begins.

1558 Elizabethan Period begins.

1600 Baroque Period begins (in Italy).

1603 Jacobean Period begins.

1666 Fire of London. Rebuilding of London by Christopher Wren.

1715 Georgian Period begins.

1750 Rococo Period begins (in France).

1811 Regency Period begins.

1837 Victorian Period begins.

1920 Modern Architecture.

Painting and Sculpture

Painting is a method of depicting scenes, or designs, on a flat surface by means of pigments. The oldest examples, found on the walls of caves, are many thousands of years old. Together with painting goes sculpture, which is the representation of objects by means of carvings, or models.

Methods of Painting

Paint consists of colouring matters (pigments) which can be mixed with a medium (water, oil, resin) and applied with a brush (or possibly fingers, sticks, or leaves, in earlier times), so that, when dry, they remain fixed to the surface used. For centuries, colours were various earths, woods, and bones burnt black and ground smoothly to a powder. Juices of plants were also used, such as indigo. In one method of painting, known as *encaustic*, waxes mixed with pigments were applied with a hot iron.

For hundreds of years the main method was that known as *fresco painting*. This was the direct application of colours to wet plaster. Areas of a wall were treated with plaster and the designs or pictures were quickly applied before the base became dry and hard.

A great advance was made when colours were mixed with fast-drying oils. Oil painting could be carried out slowly on wood (later, canvas) and changes could be made. Many great paintings are in 'oils'. From being a method of wall decoration painting became the art of separate works which could be moved from one place to another. More especially, oil paint enabled artists to depict human scenes and portraits in a more warm and natural manner.

Other methods of painting include *tempera*, in which the colours are mixed with egg-yolk, and *water-colour*.

Methods of Sculpture

At first, most sculpture was produced by carving stone, wood, or bone into the desired form. Later, sculpture was produced by moulding a form in clay over an *armature* of wood or metal. When baked, this could be used to prepare a mould from which to produce a replica of the original form in metal or cement. Modern sculptors have experimented with plastic, metals, glass, and wood to produce constructions rather than carvings.

Development of Painting

Little is known about early painting since few works survive. Broadly speaking, once artists moved from frescoes to oils a more natural art arose. Towards the end of the 13th century the work of the Italian artist Giotto inspired a new school of painters at Sienna. Fra Angelico carried this movement on, notably with a painting of *The Annunciation*. He was followed by others, especially Sandro Botticelli, who, about a century later, produced *Spring* and *The Birth of Venus*.

The great revival of learning known as the Renaissance produced many fine artists. One of the most famous paintings, the *Mona Lisa*, was produced at this time by Leonardo da Vinci.

Painting progressed through the Bolognese school, a 17th century group aiming to revive and emulate the finest of the old masters of the past, to the 18th century when elegant and romantic paintings (especially of landscapes) contrasted with paintings of great realism, often making some pointed comment on the society of the day. Notable developments in England were the works of John Constable and Joseph Turner. Both strove to render natural scenes, with special emphasis on the observed effects of light. This concern with light and natural colour was carried to the ultimate lengths by the French *Impressionists* in the 19th century. They explored the whole nature of light and abolished the use of

Above: Greek marble statue of a youth. The perfect proportions of Classical sculpture inspired many later sculptors.

Above: Michelangelo's statue of David. It shows how artists of the Renaissance were influenced by the Classical style.

Right: *Madonna, Child and St. John* by Raphael.

Portrait of a Woman with a Fan by Hals.

The Shrimp Girl by Hogarth.

The Duke of Wellington by Goya.

clear line and 'black' shadows. The invention of the photograph eventually turned the attention of artists away from purely representational painting to pure line, construction, and, eventually, abstract painting. Two important movements showed how ideas as well as forms were interesting artists. The first was *Cubism*, which aimed to break down an object and reveal many aspects of it at one and the same time. The second was *Surrealism*, which aimed to surprise, or even shock, the viewer by contrasting unlikely objects, or by depicting dream scenes.

Development of Sculpture

Sculpture was always extensively used to decorate buildings, symbol-ize beliefs and to commemorate and honour gods, kings, and leaders. The art was developed on a grand scale by the Ancient Egyptians, with their huge statues. However, their sculpture was stylized and conventional, leaving little room for free expression. The Greeks, in about 600 B.C., began to produce wonderfully realistic statues of the human form. The Romans imitated their work.

One of the greatest changes in the art was brought about by the 19th century French artist Auguste Rodin who used sculpture as a form of portraiture, and to capture movement. Modern tends to be sculpture more abstract, as in the works of Henry Moore.

Music

Music is made up of three things: *melody, harmony*, and *rhythm*.

A melody is a tune. Nearly all pieces of music contain tunes. Some are very easy to follow, such as the tune of a folk-song, or the latest recording of a 'pop' group. Others, such as the many little bits of tune in a *symphony* (piece for orchestra), may be harder.

Harmony is what we call the combined sound when several notes are played at once. A group of such notes is called a *chord*. Sometimes musicians produce a form of harmony by playing two or more tunes at once, called *counterpoint*.

Rhythm is the regular 'beat' of music. It is the simplest kind of music.

The Story of Music

Until about 1600, music was heard mainly in church, in the courts of the noblemen, at folk dances, and sing-songs. Most noblemen kept a small group of musicians to play for them privately, or publicly on such special occasions as festivals or parties. The noblemen of those days were also entertained by wandering minstrels who travelled through the country from castle to castle, singing their romantic or humorous songs to a lute or vièle accompaniment. The *lute* looked like a round-backed guitar, and the vièle was the ancestor of the violin. The Germans called these minstrels *minnesingers*, and the French called them *troubadours*.

In the 1600s, music took on a new look. Two different kinds of musical plays were developed. One kind, called *oratorio*, was religious and the other, called *opera*, dealt with non-religious subjects. The first public concert was an opera. It was performed in Italy, and this form of entertainment became popular in many parts of Europe. Of course, there had always been some music to be heard outside the church, which was sung and danced to by the ordinary people of the countryside and villages. This was folk music, which is still very much alive today.

New Instruments and New Forms

As new musical instruments were invented, and old ones improved, composers gradually began to experiment with new forms of music and try out fresh ideas. Instrumental music, as distinct from music mainly for voices, was played more and more. Antonio Stradivari was making his wonderful violins in the late 1600s and early 1700s. The piano was invented in 1709. Before this, the clavichord and the harpsichord were the most important keyboard instruments.

The 1700s were the years in which the *symphony* developed. This is a long piece of music made up of three or more *movements* (sections), usually with a pause between each. The movements are carefully designed as part of the overall plan of the symphony. *Chamber music* (music for a small group of musicians) was also greatly developed. Haydn, Mozart, and Beethoven excelled at these forms.

The early 1800s saw the rise of *romanticism* in music. This led composers, with larger orchestras and new instruments at their disposal, to write more for effects and emotion than earlier musicians. Beethoven in his nine symphonies showed that he was a master of both the romantic and the earlier style of writing called *classical*. Other composers like Schubert, Schumann and Mendelssohn continued with the romantic style.

In the later 1800s, several composers began to emphasize national characteristics in their music. The Italians concentrated on opera, in which Giuseppe Verdi was the leading composer. German opera was dominated by Richard Wagner, who wrote the words as well as the music of his

Guitar

Scottish bagpipes

Harp

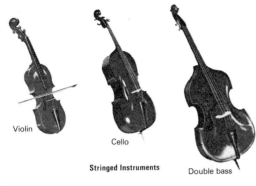

Violin

Cello

Stringed Instruments

Double bass

Clarinet

Flute

Oboe

Piccolo

Woodwind Instruments

Brass Instruments

French horn

Flugel horn

Trumpet

Percussion Instruments

Timpani
(kettledrums)

masterpieces, and called them *music dramas*. The French composer, Hector Berlioz, used new instruments and huge orchestras for his symphonies.

The 1900s have been years of searching for new forms of expression in music. Composers have experimented with strange harmonies, unusual scales, and unfamiliar rhythms. Electronic music, composed with synthesizers or the aid of sounds from tape recorders, has appeared. There are many outstanding composers today in Europe and the Americas who have contributed to various aspects of the new music. There has also been a greater interchange between the music of the West and the parallel musical cultures of China, India, and Japan, and the traditional music of Africa.

Above right: The classical ballet is a beautiful combination of music and movement.

Below right: Music and dance are both used in the service of religion. This is a temple dance from Thailand.

Atoms

Everything in the universe is made of incredibly tiny particles called atoms. Atoms are so small that if ten thousand million could be placed end to end they would measure 12.5 mm (½ inch).

At the centre of every atom lies its core or nucleus, which is very small compared with the size of the atom as a whole. Despite its small size it is in the nucleus that most of the mass of the atom is concentrated. Furthermore, the nucleus always has a positive electrical charge. At some distance from the nucleus, circling around it like planets around the Sun, are tiny, very light particles called *electrons*. These electrons are negatively charged and are held in orbit by the attraction between their own negative charge and the positive charge of the nucleus.

The nucleus contains small heavy particles called *protons*, which possess the positive charge, and other small particles called *neutrons* which have the same mass as the protons but have no charge at all.

Atomic Number

The electrons have just as much negative charge as the protons have positive charge, although the protons are almost 2,000 times heavier. Because the negative charge of one electron exactly cancels the positive charge of one proton, the number of protons in the nucleus must be equal to the number of electrons in orbit for the atom as a whole to remain neutral. The number of protons possessed by any atom is called its *atomic* or *proton number* and there are usually at least as many neutrons as there are protons in the nucleus of an atom. Hydrogen is the only atom with no neutrons.

We might expect an atom of helium (atomic number 2) to be twice as heavy as an atom of hydrogen (atomic

Above: A hydrogen atom consists of a single electron moving round a single proton. The orbit of the electron changes rapidly.

Above: The orbit of the electron is shown as a solid shell, cut away to reveal the proton.

Below: An oxygen atom has eight protons and eight neutrons in its nucleus. Eight electrons circle the nucleus.

number 1) but it is in fact four times as heavy. This extra heaviness (mass) is of course due to the presence of two neutrons in the nucleus of helium. Since the proton is very small and the electron even smaller, it can be seen that the atom consists largely of space with most of its mass concentrated at the centre. (Although atoms are pictured as a billiard-ball type of sphere, it must be remembered there is no solid shell like this around them.)

In atom number 3, lithium (symbol Li), three electrons orbit around a nucleus containing three protons and four neutrons. By adding the total numbers of protons and neutrons we see that an atom of lithium is seven times as heavy as an atom of hydrogen. In other words, the *relative atomic mass* of lithium is seven. Atom number 6 is carbon (symbol C). Its nucleus is made up of six protons and six neutrons, giving it a relative atomic mass of twelve. The six positive charges on the protons are balanced by six negatively charged electrons circling the nucleus.

The electron orbits in every atom are

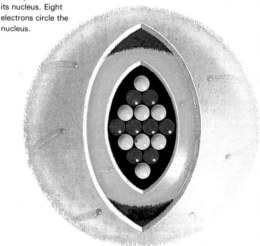

Far right: Below 1,080°C, copper is a solid. Its atoms are closely packed and vibrate together while remaining in their fixed pattern.

Right: Between 1,080°C and 2,580°C, copper is a liquid. The atoms are still tightly packed but they slip against each other in all directions, and so a liquid has no shape.

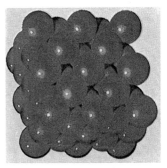

arranged in a series of shells. The innermost shell can hold no more than two electrons and the second shell can hold no more than eight. The heavier atoms have more shells.

Elements

If we could separate all the atoms in the Universe we should find there are over 90 different kinds. A substance whose atoms are all of one kind is called an *element*.

In an element atoms are held together by mutual attraction. In a *solid* this attraction is strong. In a *liquid* it is weak. In a *gas* the atoms move freely. Heating can weaken the attraction between atoms, changing an element from solid to liquid, and then to gas.

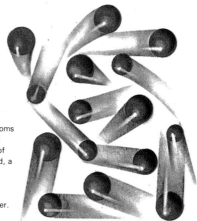

Right: Above 2,580°C, copper is a gas. The atoms are moving so fast that they have broken free of each other. Like a liquid, a gas has no shape, but, unlike a liquid, it will spread out to fill completely any container.

Fuel for Power

All the common fuels we burn to provide heat and power come from the ground. Coal, petroleum, and natural gas were all formed millions of years ago deep down in the Earth from decayed plant and animal matter. These fuels are really 'stored sunlight', because the plants needed the Sun's energy to grow and the animals needed the plants as food. They are often called *fossil fuels*. Wood, too, is an important fuel, especially in many of the developing countries.

Above: Laying a pipeline to carry natural gas across the country.

Oil Prospecting

There was a time when oil was discovered almost by accident, a slight seepage of oil on the ground indicating the presence of large or small deposits far underground. Today more scientific methods are used.

The instrument most used is the *seismograph*, which is also used to detect and measure the strengths of distant earthquakes. A seismograph is basically a small pendulum which moves when the ground vibrates. In *seismic oil prospecting* a number of small seismographs are placed in the ground over a wide area. These instruments contain special devices (similar to a microphone) which transmit a vibrating electric current to a portable control station when the ground vibrates.

A charge of dynamite is set off in the area, and the seismographs measure the resulting vibrations in the ground. Some of these may go deep down into the ground and be reflected back to the surface, where the seismographs can detect and measure this underground 'reflection'. Depending upon the measurements the geologists can decide whether or not the underground layers reflecting back the vibrations are likely to contain oil deposits.

Below: A great deal of natural gas is found under the sea bed. Huge drilling rigs are erected in the sea to bore down and tap deposits of natural gas.

Oil Wells

The main feature of an oil well is the *derrick*, a tall metal framework supporting a block and tackle holding up the drill pipe. This is a hollow steel rod which carries the *drill bit*, a diamond-studded toothed steel cone which can gnaw its way through solid rock. At ground level the drill rod is clamped to a circular steel *table*, which turns the drill rod. As the drill gradually moves downwards it is periodically hoisted back to the surface by the block and tackle, and a fresh section of drill rod is connected. In time the drill rod may extend in sections to depths of 3,000 metres (10,000 feet).

The rock powder which is produced by the rotating drill bit is brought to the surface by pumping down a mixture of soft mud and water through the central hole in the drill pipe. This mud and water mixture returns to the surface in the space between the drill pipe and the hole which has been drilled.

When oil is struck the derrick is removed and the gushing well is plugged with a complicated system of

valves called a *christmas tree*. This is connected with the pipelines which carry the oil to the refinery or to a port for loading into tanker ships.

Oil Refining

The dark brown thick liquid which comes from an oil well must be refined before it can be used. A modern oil refinery consists of two main types of equipment. The *fractionating columns* are vertical steel cylinders in which the oil is heated so that the various liquids it contains are boiled off. Their vapours are then condensed back at different temperatures, so that they become separated from one another.

These liquids in turn are then placed in *crackers*, large steel tanks where

Above: When coal-burning steam engines powered industry and rail transport, coal was often moved by canal.

Right: Much coal is carried by railway trucks. The railway may come directly to the pithead, where the trucks are loaded with coal.

Below: A miner working with a cutting machine at a coal face deep underground.

further separation takes place under the influence of heat and pressure and the use of *catalysts*. These are substances which cause chemical reactions to take place. The oil is broken down into various useful fuels such as benzene, paraffin (kerosene), petrol (gasoline), various oils used for lubricating, diesel fuel, and fuel oil for use in heating homes and factories.

Natural Gas

By drilling down into the ground we can secure not only petroleum but *natural gas*, which is a mixture of compounds of carbon and hydrogen such as methane, ethane, propane, and butane.

In many countries natural gas is replacing coal gas as a source of power. The gas can be liquefied under pressure and transported from the gas fields in *tankers*. Arriving at its port of destination, the gas is vapourized and flows through long pipelines to the towns and cities where it is to be used.

Coal

The coal we use today comes from trees and plants which grew more than two hundred million years ago. When these trees and plants died they were buried under layers of sand and loose rock. Increasing pressure and heat caused hydrogen and oxygen to be squeezed out in the form of water, carbon dioxide, and other gases, leaving a very high proportion of carbon.

Coal occurs underground in layers, or *seams*, which sometimes slope upwards to form *outcrops* at the surface. Here the coal can be quarried out directly by *open cast* mining. Most coal, however, is obtained by excavating shafts down to the seam.

A modern coal mine, or *colliery*, has at least two shafts to ensure proper ventilation. At the top, or *head*, of one shaft fans ensure a good circulation of air. A derrick, or *head gear*, at the surface lowers a cage down into the shaft. This is used to carry miners to their work and bring up the mined coal.

From the shaft the miners dig along the seam, cutting coal from the *face*, loading it into small cars which run on rails back to the shaft, where they are carried to the surface. Today many mines are equipped with long conveyor belts to carry the coal, and the coal itself can be cut from the face with automatic cutting machines. The roof is held up by beams supported by adjustable *pit-props* to prevent cave-ins.

Nuclear Fuel

An increasingly important source of power is nuclear energy. The principal 'fuel' used is uranium. The uranium is placed in a plant called a *reactor*. There, the nuclei of its atoms are split. When this happens enormous amounts of energy are released, mainly as heat

Above: Scientists detect oil beneath the ground by exploding small charges and registering the patterns of shock waves produced.

Below: An oil refinery seen through a heat haze caused by burning waste gases.

(see pages 106–107). This heat can be used in the same way as burning other fuels to generate electricity. By the early 1980s, more than 3 per cent of the world's electricity was generated by nuclear power plants. A nuclear power plant uses much less fuel than one burning fossil fuels. For example, one tonne of uranium produces as much power as 12 million barrels of oil.

Chemistry

All substances are chemicals. The study of chemistry is the study of every substance, its structure, its composition and the reactions in which it takes part.

The overwhelming variety of materials occurring in nature are made up from ninety-two basic ingredients called *elements*.

Each element contains atoms of one size only. An atom is defined as the smallest part of an element which shows the chemical properties of that element. Atoms join together to form what we call *molecules*. The number of groups which can be arranged out of 92 distinct atoms is almost incalculable. A substance built up chemically from more than one element is called a *compound*.

Branches of Chemistry

Nearly half a million compounds are known to contain the element carbon, and they are given a branch of chemistry to themselves called *organic chemistry*. The name comes from the carbon compounds produced by living organisms. The study of elements other than carbon is called *inorganic chemistry*. A third great division is that concerned with the structure of matter and the laws governing chemical reactions. It is called *physical chemistry*, a name which rightly suggests the application of both physics and chemistry. Analytical chemistry is concerned with the identification of the various ingredients of a compound (*qualitative analysis*) and finding out the quantity of each present (*quantitative analysis*).

Chemical Compounds

If crystals of sugar could be ground into particles smaller than those of the finest talcum powder, they would still behave as sugar. We believe that the smallest particle that can show the behaviour of sugar is the sugar *molecule*. This can be broken down further only into *atoms* of carbon, hydrogen, and oxygen. Sugar is a *compound*; carbon, hydrogen, and oxygen are its *elements*.

In describing a chemical change or 'reaction' it is convenient to employ symbols and formulae instead of writing the names in full. Each of the elements is represented by one or two letters: for example, H = hydrogen, O = oxygen, Na = sodium, Cl = chlorine. A molecule of common salt consists of an atom of sodium joined to an atom of chlorine, so its symbol is NaCl.

Above: Different elements are made of different atoms, the difference being in the numbers of protons and neutrons in the nucleus and the number of orbiting electrons.

Below: Servicing a chemical reaction vessel.

Heat

If you put a pan on a fire or a stove, it soon gets hot. It does not look any different, but something has obviously happened to it. If you could see the molecules, the small particles that make up the pan, you would find that they were moving about more vigorously than when the pan was cold. In this way, you would see that heat is a form of energy, and that it takes the form of molecular motion.

Temperature

The hotness or coldness of things is called their *temperature*. Instruments called *thermometers* measure temperature. People measure temperature in units called *degrees*: the more degrees, the higher the temperature. For most scientific purposes the temperature at which water turns to ice is called 0

Above: All substances contain a certain amount of heat, even ice. If a container of liquid oxygen is placed on a block of ice, the oxygen will boil back to a gas. Liquid oxygen has a boiling point of − 183°C, whereas ice has a temperature around 0°C. Heat flows from the ice into the liquid oxygen.

degrees, and the normal temperature at which water boils is 100 degrees. This is the Celsius scale, named after its inventor, Anders Celsius, a Swedish scientist, and sometimes called the Centigrade scale.

Some people use another scale, called the Fahrenheit scale, after its inventor, Daniel Fahrenheit. On this scale water freezes at 32 degrees and normally boils at 212 degrees. The lowest temperature, called Absolute Zero, is minus 460 degrees on the Fahrenheit scale, or about minus 273 degrees on the Celsius scale.

Movement of Heat

Heat can travel in three ways: by *radiation*, by *convection*, and by *conduction*. In radiation, heat travels through space, as it does from the Sun or a fire. In convection, it travels through moving water—as in a central heating system—or moving air, as

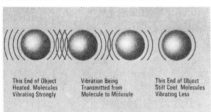

This End of Object Heated. Molecules Vibrating Strongly

Vibration Being Transmitted from Molecule to Molecule

This End of Object Still Cool. Molecules Vibrating Less

Above: How heat travels by conduction. As one end of an object is heated, the molecules at that point vibrate strongly, and this vibration is transmitted through the object.

Right: A water-heating system. Cold water, heated in a boiler, rises through convection and is stored in the hot water tank. Cool water from the bottom of the hot water tank returns to the boiler to be reheated. When hot water is drawn off, more water enters the system from the cold water tank.

Left: Black bodies absorb and therefore radiate more heat than white bodies. This is why white clothes are worn in the Tropics.

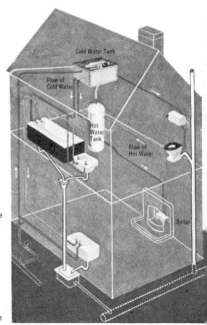

Cold Water Tank

Flow of Cold Water

Hot Water Tank

Flow of Hot Water

Boiler

from a convector heater. In conduction, heat travels through a substance as, for example, along a metal rod when one end of it is held in a flame.

Heat travels very slowly through some substances. These are said to be *insulators*. Examples of good insulators include wood, bricks, and paper.

Many things change when they are heated. Metals *expand*, that is, they grow slightly larger in size. Air also expands when it is heated. Hot air is used to fill balloons, because it is lighter than the cold air around it. Water expands when heated. A full kettle overflows when the water in it gets hot. Very hot water becomes steam, which expands very greatly.

Solids, Liquids, and Gases

When heat is applied to a solid, it can either go to raising its temperature or to melting it. Heat which raises the temperature does so by making the solid molecules *vibrate*, or move faster. This kind of energy is called *kinetic* energy, which means energy of motion. If heat is continually supplied

to a solid, its molecules vibrate more and more until eventually they 'fall apart' and the solid melts. In a similar way, heated liquid eventually boils and becomes a gas or vapour. Heat which changes the state of a substance from a solid to a liquid, or from a liquid to a gas, is called *latent heat.*

Measuring Temperature

Thermometers are instruments that measure the temperature of an object. Every change brought about by heating can be used to measure temperature. An obvious change is the *expansion* or increase in size, which most objects undergo when they get hotter.

The *mercury thermometer* makes use of expansion. It consists of a fine glass tube connected to a bulb containing mercury. As the temperature rises, the mercury expands and rises along the tube. The position of the mercury against a scale of degrees marked on the glass tube indicates the temperature.

One kind of electrical thermometer uses the principle of the *thermocouple*, a device that generates electricity when it is heated. Temperatures are indicated by the voltage generated. Another electrical thermometer, the *platinum resistance thermometer*, indicates temperatures in terms of the resistance of a piece of platinum wire.

Electricity

An electric current is a movement, or flow, of minute particles called *electrons*. Normally, electrons are attached to an atom and circle round its central nucleus in orbits—just like artificial satellites orbiting the Earth. Each electron has the same charge or 'packet' of electricity described as a *negative* charge. Usually the nucleus has exactly enough *positive* electrical charges to balance the negative charges on the electrons, so that the atom as a whole is neutral.

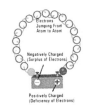

Above: An electric current is a flow of electrons which jump from atom to atom when there is a difference of electrical 'pressure' (voltage) between the ends of a wire.

In some materials, however, a few of the electrons in each atom are only loosely held. These *free electrons* can jump from atom to atom, and it is a steady drift of free electrons that carries electricity through a wire.

When some kind of 'driving force' is applied to the wire, the wandering electrons are organized into a steady one-way drift. The driving force is simply a difference of electrical 'pressure' (voltage) between the ends of the wire. It is provided by either a battery or generator. Electrical 'pressure' starts the drift of electrons by pushing the loosely held electrons

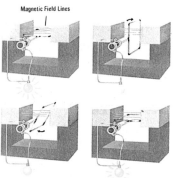

Left: A simple generator. As the wire loop is moved through a magnetic field, a voltage is set up in it and a current flows through it. The current is greatest when the loop is cutting *across* the lines of force and least when it is moving *along* the lines of force.

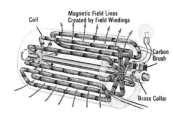

Above: A practical generator has a number of coils of wire to minimize the current fluctuations. The magnetic field is produced by electromagnets. Carbon brushes collect the electricity generated.

Below: In a power station, heat energy is converted to electrical energy. The heat is used to turn water to steam. The steam drives a turbine which turns the armature of a generator.

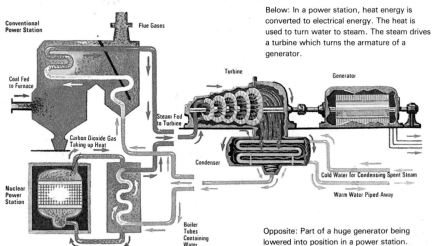

Opposite: Part of a huge generator being lowered into position in a power station.

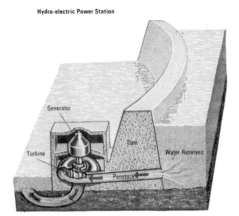

Hydro-electric Power Station

from the first atom in the line to the next, and so on.

A current of electricity must have a completely unbroken path, or *circuit*. Wires which carry an electric current are often made of copper. Copper, like most metals, is a good *conductor* of electricity. It has plenty of free electrons, so a current has little difficulty in travelling through it. Materials such as rubber and plastics are good *insulators* (bad conductors). Their atoms do not have any loosely held electrons. When an electric current flows through a conductor that offers resistance to its flow it heats the conductor. If the conductor is made of suitable *resistance* wire it glows red and gives off a good heat. This is the principle used in electric fires. If the right type of resistance is chosen it glows white hot and provides light.

Generating Electricity

Electricity is generated by *alternators*. These machines make use of the fact that when a wire moves through a magnetic field a voltage is set up, or *induced*, in the wire. In an alternator the wires are arranged in a circle around a rotating shaft called the *armature*. Connection is made with the armature through metal rings on the shaft which make contact with two

Above: In a hydro-electric power station, water rushing out from the base of a dam is directed on to the blades of a turbine, causing it to revolve. The turbine drives a generator.

Above: When an electric current flows through a conductor which offers resistance to its flow, the conductor becomes hot. This is the principle used in the electric light bulb. A coil of fine wire with a high resistance glows white-hot as an electric current passes through it.

fixed *carbon brushes*. As the wires rotate they move downwards through the magnetic field and then upwards. This means that the direction of the induced voltage keeps changing—it is an alternating voltage.

Direct voltage can be obtained by fitting a *commutator* instead of slip rings. This device keeps reversing the voltage to compensate for the natural reversals. Machines of this type are called *dynamos*.

Electric Motors

Direct current electric motors are constructed in the same way as dynamos. When they are switched on the electric current flows through the wires around the armature setting up a magnetic field around them. This field interacts with the main field of the rotor causing the wires on one side to be forced down and those on the other side to be forced up. This causes the armature to rotate and drive anything connected to the motor. Alternating current motors are constructed in a slightly different way, but work on the same principle.

Chemical and Static Electricity

Batteries generate electric current through chemical action. A popular type, the *dry cell*, uses a zinc case containing ammonium chloride in the centre of which is a carbon rod surrounded by a mixture of manganese dioxide and carbon. Chemical action in the battery leaves the carbon rod positively charged and the zinc case negatively charged. The familiar *static electricity* effect occurs when an object such as a comb is given an excess of electrons, or if a number of them are removed. It then becomes either negatively or positively charged. Positively and negatively charged objects will attract each other. Two positively or two negatively charged objects will repel each other.

Magnetism

Magnetism owes its name to the fact that the early Greeks found the natural magnetic material called lodestone in an area called Magnesia. Lodestone, like man-made magnets, has several very interesting properties. For one thing it attracts pieces of iron. For another, when mounted so it can swing freely lodestone always points towards the North Pole of the Earth, and can be used to help find direction, for example out at sea.

Materials owe their magnetism to the way in which the electrons of their atoms are arranged. In some materials, such as lodestone, iron and steel, the arrangements of the electrons are such that the individual molecules of the material are each a tiny magnet. At one end of each molecule there is what is known as a north-seeking pole.

In a natural piece of iron, the individual molecules lie in many different directions and the bar of iron

Above: One property of a magnet is that it attracts pieces of iron to it.

Above: A compass needle is a small bar magnet which is allowed to swing freely. It always comes to rest with one end pointing towards the Earth's magnetic north pole.

Right: Every magnet has two poles, a north and a south. The unlike poles of two magnets attract each other.

Right: The like poles of two magnets repel each other.

Bottom right: When an electric current is passed through a coil of wire, the coil behaves like a bar magnet. The strength of the magnetic field can be increased by placing a soft iron core inside the coil. Coil and core are together known as an electromagnet.

itself does not point in any particular direction.

To convert the bar of iron into a compass needle we need only stroke the south pole of an existing magnet along its length. As it moves along, the south pole will cause the north poles of all the molecules to swing round and point towards it. By the time it reaches the far end of the bar, many of the molecules will be pointing in the same direction. The whole bar will now act as the individual molecules do, only in a much more powerful manner. The bar of iron has become a magnet.

From this behaviour we can see that a south pole will attract a north pole. Similarly, a north pole will attract a south pole. However, two south poles or two north poles repel each other.

We can also make a piece of iron or steel into a magnet by wrapping a coil of wire round it and connecting the coil to a direct current supply. When the current flows through the coil it will set up a magnetic field, just like that of a real magnet, and this will pull the molecules into line. This is called electromagnetism.

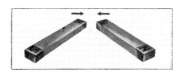

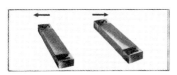

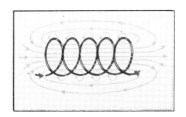

Above: The Earth acts as though it contained a vast bar magnet. One end of a compass needle always comes to rest pointing to the Earth's magnetic north pole. The magnetic north and south poles do not correspond to the geographic north and south poles, a fact which must be taken into account with compass readings. Moreover, the position of the magnetic poles changes over the years.

Light

Light is a form of energy, as heat and sound are. Our eyes are sensitive to light, and we see things because light is reflected from them. If there is no light, we cannot see. Light is produced whenever an object gets extremely hot. For instance, if we heat a poker in a fire, it first gets red hot and gives off a feeble red light. Then it gets yellow, and finally it glows white hot. A white-hot object giving off light is said to be *incandescent*. The wire filament inside an electric lamp becomes incandescent and gives off light when an electric current passes through it. A candle flame contains particles of carbon which become incandescent and give off light. The Sun is a fiery ball of incandescent gas.

Light travels more or less in straight lines. It will not go round corners and for this reason objects exposed to a single strong source of light cast shadows. Light travels by radiation. To a scientist, it is a form of radiant energy and is closely related to heat rays, X-rays, and even radio waves.

The Nature of Light

Early scientists believed that light is made up of millions of tiny particles called *corpuscles* travelling at enormous speeds. Reflection of a ray of light by a mirror seemed to support this theory;

Above: Lights blaze at an oil refinery by night. Below: The rival theories of the nature of light: the corpuscular theory and the wave theory. Both are now believed to be partly correct. Light consists of 'packets' of energy which travel as waves.

they thought that each corpuscle 'bounced' off the surface of the mirror in much the same way that a rubber ball bounces off a wall. The angle at which a ray of light strikes a mirror (the angle of *incidence*) is exactly the same as the angle at which it is reflected back (the angle of *reflection*).

Another theory is that light consists of waves. According to the wave theory, light radiates out from its source as a series of waves—rather like the ripples in the surface of a pond spreading out from a stone's splash. Light waves can be thought of as consisting of a succession of crests and troughs. The distance between any two successive crests (or troughs) is called the *wavelength* of the light. These are very small—a few millionths of a centimetre. The number of waves passing a point in space every second is the *frequency* of the light.

According to modern quantum theory, all kinds of radiation consist of

---

Electromagnetic Radiation

Light, ultra-violet, infra-red rays, radio waves, and X-rays, are all forms of *electromagnetic radiation*, and differ only in their wavelengths, measured in nanometres (nm).

All forms of electromagnetic energy can be arranged in order of wavelength in the *electromagnetic spectrum*. Visible light ranges from about 760 nm for red light to about 400 nm for violet light. Infra-red or 'heat' rays are longer than red light in wavelength and are invisible. Ultra-violet, X-rays, and Gamma rays have shorter wavelengths than violet light and can only be detected using special photographic films. Much longer again than infra-red rays are short, medium, and long radio waves.

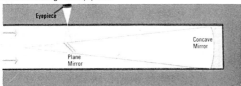

In a refracting telescope, the object lens forms an image which is observed through the eyepiece.

Newtonian form of reflecting telescope. An image formed by the concave mirror is observed through the side of the telescope.

Cassegrain form of reflecting telescope. An image formed by the concave mirror is observed through the end of the telescope.

Telescopes

There are two chief kinds of telescopes, *refracting telescopes* and *reflecting telescopes*. Refracting telescopes consist of a tube with a convex lens at one end and a concave lens at the other. The convex lens is called the *objective lens*. The concave lens is called the *eyepiece*. The objective lens collects light from the object, and forms a small image of it inside the tube. The eyepiece then magnifies it.

In the reflecting telescope, a concave mirror collects light from the object and reflects it on to a flat mirror, which reflects it to the eyepiece.

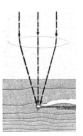

Right: A double convex lens brings together light rays which pass through it so that they meet at the focus. A burning glass is a double convex lens. It concentrates a beam of sunlight to a point.

tiny 'packets' of energy called *quanta* which travel as waves. A quantum of light is called a *photon*, and it corresponds in many ways to the early corpuscles. Photons travel as waves—and so the wave theory is also basically correct.

The Speed of Light

Light travels at the fastest speed known. In a vacuum or in outer space, light travels at about 300,000 km (186,000 miles) a second. In air or water or glass, light travels more slowly. The denser the medium, the slower it travels. This slowing down bends the light waves slightly, and so a light ray passing at an angle into water or glass is bent. This bending is called *refraction* and it is how lenses focus beams of light.

The frequency of light also determines its colour. For example, red light has a lower frequency than has blue light. White light is a mixture of all frequencies.

Above: Refraction can be demonstrated by the 'cup and coin' trick. Place a coin at the bottom of a cup so that it is just out of sight. If you fill the cup with water, you can see the coin. This is because light rays from the coin have been bent at the surface of the water.

Above: When 'white' light passes through a prism it is split into violet, indigo, blue, green, yellow, orange, and red. Below: Objects appear coloured because they absorb part of the light falling upon them and reflect the remainder.

103

The World of Sound

Sound is energy in the form of *vibrations* which can be detected by the ears. These vibrations, which are movements to and fro of air, are called *sound waves*. They travel through the air and make the eardrums vibrate also. Nerves sense the eardrums' vibrations and send messages to the brain, and so we hear the sound.

When an object such as a guitar string or door bell vibrates, we pick up the sound waves almost immediately. But if we watch a man chopping wood in the distance, we see the axe hit the wood before we hear the sound of the blow. This is because light travels

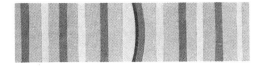

Sound waves consist of regions of varying pressure produced in the air when objects vibrate. As a guitar string (black) is plucked it vibrates at a constant rate in the air (grey). As it moves, it produces a region of high pressure ahead (dark grey) and a region of low pressure behind (light grey).

Below: A reel to reel stereophonic tape recorder.

Tape Recording

Sound recordings on tape are used more and more in place of ordinary records. In making a recording, sound waves are converted into a varying electric current by a microphone. This current is fed into the tape recorder where it is amplified and passed on to the recording head. The head is an electromagnet with a narrow gap cut into it. The magnetic field in the gap varies with the microphone current. Plastic tape coated with iron oxide is drawn across the gap at a steady speed and is magnetized by the varying field. Each particle of iron oxide becomes a permanent magnet with a strength proportional to the size of current flowing in the head at the instant when that particle was in the magnetic field.

To play back the recording, the tape is drawn past the playback head at the same steady speed. In effect we have a series of tiny magnets (the tape) moving near to a coil (the head) which produces a current of electricity in the coil. This current varies with the strength of the 'magnets' and is therefore a replica of the original microphone current. After amplification it goes through a loudspeaker to reproduce the original sound. If the recording is no longer required the tape can be 'wiped clean' by passing it over an erase head which produces a rapidly alternating magnetic field that demagnetizes the tape.

Right: Compass needles are deflected near a magnet.
Far right: In a magnetic tape, the particles of iron oxide act as tiny compass needles. As the tape passes the magnets in a tape recorder, the particles are magnetized; their magnetic poles are deflected in the same way forming a magnetic pattern in the tape.

faster than sound. Sound waves in air travel at 331 metres (1,087 feet) a second. Sound travels faster through *denser* materials such as water and metal. Sound cannot travel at all in a vacuum because there is no *medium* (substance) to carry the vibrations.

We can tell one sound from another by its *pitch, loudness,* and *quality.* The vibrations of a low-pitched note are slower than those of a high note. The number of the vibrations per second is called the *frequency.*

Loudness is the apparent intensity of sound which we hear. Noises may not sound equally loud to different people because people's ears are not equally sensitive.

The farther away from the sound source you are, the quieter the sound seems, because the energy decreases as it travels outwards.

The quality of sounds differs because almost all noises are made up of more than one frequency. When an object vibrates, its parts vibrate at the same time, producing a mixture of frequencies. Each half, third or quarter of a cello string, for instance, may vibrate separately, giving notes at a higher pitch, though with less energy. It is these additional vibrations, called *harmonics*, which add to the interest of the sound and give it its characteristic tone quality. Noise is produced by an irregular mixture of vibrations; musical notes are regular, ordered vibrations.

The pitch of a sound depends on its wavelength (the distance between one high-pressure region and the next) and the frequency at which the pressure regions arrive. The deep sound of a double bass has a long wavelength and a low frequency (1). The high-pitched sound of a flute has a short wavelength and a high frequency (2). In soft sounds, such as a violin makes, the amplitude of the sound waves is small (3). A jet engine produces large-amplitude waves, and a low sound (4).

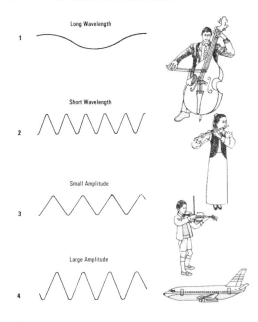

The Telephone The telephone has both a microphone and an earpiece. A voice speaking into the microphone causes the diaphragm to vibrate. As it does so, carbon granules behind it are in turn compressed and released. An electric current passing through them is affected by this, and its variation corresponds to the vibrations of the diaphragm. The earpiece consists of an electromagnet and a metallic diaphragm. The current energizes the magnet, which pulls the diaphragm towards it. Variations in the current make the diaphragm move to and fro, setting up sound waves.

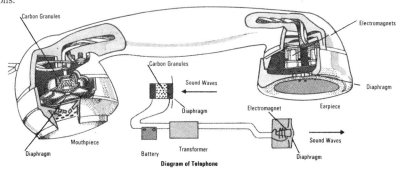

Nuclear Power

The nucleus of the atom consists of particles called protons and neutrons, held together by powerful attractive forces. When the nucleus is broken to pieces, there is a change in mass which appears as energy in the form of heat and radiation. In 1932 Sir John Cockcroft and E. T. S. Walton 'split' atoms of lithium by 'bombarding' them with protons. The protons, being positive electrically, were speeded up by being attracted down metal tubes which were charged negatively. At the bottom of the tubes was placed a piece of lithium metal. This apparatus was one of the first *particle accelerators* or 'atom smashers'.

One of the most modern types of atom smashers is the *synchrotron*. The walls of a huge circular tube are lined with powerful magnets, whose 'field of force' keeps the bombarding particles in the centre of the tube. The particles are whirled around the tube at ever increasing speeds by a high-frequency alternating current.

Above: The synchrotron is one kind of *particle accelerator* — an atom-smashing machine. Protons are fed into the synchrotron from a high-energy source such as a Van der Graaff generator or a linear accelerator. The protons are accelerated in the synchrotron by a radio frequency accelerator and kept in a circular path by the action of the ring of magnets.

Below: In the AGR (advanced gas-cooled reactor) the reactor is cooled by carbon dioxide gas. The hot gas goes to heat exchangers where the heat turns water into steam to drive turbines connected to electrical generators. The concrete biological shield protects workers from dangerous radiation.

The Chain Reaction

When an atomic bomb explodes, a vast amount of energy is released in a tiny fraction of a second. In the bomb, the energy that was locked up in the nuclei of uranium atoms is released when these nuclei are split up. This *fission reaction* is triggered off by the capture of a neutron by a single uranium nucleus. The nucleus breaks up, throwing out a number of fragments, neutrons among them. These neutrons are captured by more uranium nuclei which then split up producing another generation containing still more neutrons. The process repeats itself until the whole mass of uranium is consumed. In this *chain reaction* a vast amount of energy is created using quite a small mass of uranium.

The atomic explosion is an example of an *uncontrolled fission reaction*, with all the energy released in as short a time as possible. To drive power stations, a steady source of energy is needed, and this may be obtained from a *controlled* fission reaction. In this, the uranium 'fuel' must be consumed slowly and steadily. The energy of the exploding nuclear fragments is then converted into heat energy, which is carried away and used to turn water into steam to drive the turbines. This process is carried out in a nuclear *reactor*, or *pile*.

Using Uranium

Every pile uses nuclear fuel—a material that will support the controlled chain reaction. The fuel most commonly used in nuclear reactors is uranium. Naturally occurring uranium is a mixture of different isotopes (atoms of the same element but of different masses). Over 99% of the naturally found element is uranium-238, and less than 1% is the lighter isotope, uranium-235. Uranium-235 is most useful in promoting a chain reaction, and to make atomic bombs, great expense and trouble was incurred in extracting the lighter isotope.

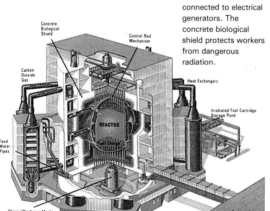

Concrete Biological Shield

Control Rod Mechanism

Carbon Dioxide Gas

Heat Exchangers

Irradiated Fuel Cartridge Storage Pond

REACTOR

Feed Water Pipes

Fuel Charge

Charge/Discharge Machine on Rails and Turntable

Turbine Hall

For use in nuclear reactors it would be obviously easier and cheaper to be able to use uranium in its naturally occurring form. To do this, the pile has to be constructed so that fission of the uranium-235 occurs, while the uranium-238 is not allowed to interfere with the process. A large block of graphite has holes drilled in it. In these holes are placed a number of *fuel rods* which are made of uranium-238 which also contains a small proportion of the 'explosive' atoms of uranium-235. These keep on splitting and giving off energy within the uranium-238 and heat is produced in the graphite block.

As the uranium-235 atoms split, very fast-moving neutrons are produced. Uranium-238 absorbs fast- but not slow-moving neutrons, so to keep the 'reaction' going the fast neutrons are

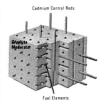

Above: In the core of a uranium-graphite pile, uranium fuel elements are placed in loading tubes separated by blocks of graphite moderator. Cadmium control rods may be pushed in or out.

Below: C-Stellarator, used in the United States for thermonuclear research.

slowed down when they pass through the graphite block, called a *moderator*. Now the uranium-238 will not absorb the neutrons, which can freely move about among the uranium-235 atoms, bombarding them so that they will keep on splitting as a 'controlled' chain reaction.

Thermonuclear Power

Just as the *fission* of heavy atomic nuclei releases energy, so does the *fusion* of light atomic nuclei. The fusion of hydrogen is the Sun's chief source of energy. Fusion, or *thermonuclear*, reactions are a promising source of power. Deuterium, an isotope of hydrogen, is used as the starting point for man-made nuclear fusions since it is easier to fuse than ordinary hydrogen.

Rail Transport

Until the 1800s, transport by land was desperately slow. Roads were in a terrible condition, and travel by stage-coach was both uncomfortable and unreliable. Then, in 1803, the British engineer Richard Trevithick, thought of mounting the newly developed steam carriage on rails to provide a smoother ride. A year later he demonstrated the first rail locomotive. The idea of 'railways' was not new, however. Horse-drawn railways were being used in most large mines at the time.

The first railway line—the Stockton and Darlington colliery line—was opened in northern England in 1825. The first passenger line, the Liverpool and Manchester Railway, opened in 1830.

From then on, development was rapid. As early as the 1850s it was possible to travel by train through several European countries. Soon, lines were opened all over the world. With the growth of railways, goods and raw materials could be moved speedily between mines and factories, towns and ports. Towns began to spring up in previously uninhabited regions.

Nowhere was the impact of the railways greater than on the vast continent of North America. After the American Civil War, work started

Above: On Japan's New Tokkaido line trains travel at over 160 kph (100 mph).
Left: The world's first public railway opened September 25, 1825. George Stephenson's *Locomotion* hauled 33 wagons at 16 kph (10 mph) between Stockton and Darlington.
Below: Rail journeys across the USA became possible in 1869, when railways from east and west met in Utah.

from both sides of the continent on the 'Great American Railway' from the Pacific to the Atlantic coasts. In 1869 the two sections met.

Locomotive Design

The Railway Age was made possible by the steam locomotive. Today, many countries have changed to electric or diesel locomotives which are cheaper and cleaner to run. But the steam loco-motive is a much simpler piece of machinery, and it will be some years before it is replaced everywhere.

In a steam locomotive coal or oil is burned in the *firebox* and tubes carry

the smoke and hot gases through a boiler where water changes to steam. The steam forces *pistons* back and forth in the *cylinders*. The pistons are linked to the *driving wheels* by *connecting rods*. The fuel and water for the firebox are carried in a towed tender.

Electric locomotives are driven by electric motors connected to the driving wheels. The current to power the motors is picked up either from a conductor rail or an overhead wire. An electric locomotive is a highly efficient machine. It needs no preparation for service. It can accelerate rapidly, haul very heavy loads, and also run at high speed over long distances.

Diesel locomotives are classified according to the way in which the power from the engine is transmitted to the wheels. In the *diesel-electric* type, the engines turn generators which produce electricity. The electricity powers motors to drive the wheels. The *diesel-mechanical* type has the same type of transmission system (clutch and gearbox) as a road vehicle. The *diesel-hydraulic* type has an automatic fluid transmission.

For short- and medium-distance passenger services, diesel or electric power units are often built into train sets consisting of two, three, or four coaches permanently coupled together with a driving cab at each end. If a longer train is required, two or more train sets can be coupled together.

Modern Railways

Railways are now being modernized throughout the world in order to meet competition from road and air transport. Track-laying and maintenance are now highly mechanized. Rails are being welded together to make continuous lengths for smoother running. Built-in automatic warning systems on the track and in the locomotives help to prevent crashes. Signalling is by swift, push-button control.

Above: The Victoria line, a new underground railway beneath London, opened in 1969.

Above: The monorail is a current development in rail transport. This one in Tokyo runs on top of a rail with wheels on either side to steady it.

Underground Railways

Many cities have electric railways which run below ground in the central area and may come out into the open in the suburbs. In North America they are called *subways*. In some countries they are called *Metros*, after the first Metropolitan Railway.

Underground railways are valuable in cities where they take a huge volume of traffic off the streets. They are especially used by people commuting to and from work.

The tunnels are often close to the surface, and are made by digging a large trench and roofing it. Some systems also have deep-level tunnels which are bored through the ground. In London, deep-level tunnels form a group called the 'tubes'.

Trains are multiple units, with automatic sliding doors. They usually have plenty of standing room because journeys are short and the trains are very crowded at times.

An automatic colour-light signalling system is used with only short sections between which enables the trains to follow each other quickly. At the stations, moving staircases, or *escalators*, cope with the periodic flood of passengers from the trains. Some stations even have moving footpaths to speed the flow.

The world's first underground railway was the 'Metropolitan Railway' opened in London in 1863. In 1890 the first deep-level 'tube' was opened, running beneath the River Thames. London's underground system is still the world's largest, with about 400 km (240 miles) of route including 110 km (70 miles) of bored tunnel. The New York system, opened in 1904, is almost as large and even more compact. It carries more than 1,600 million passengers a year.

The Paris Métro was opened in 1900. Its trains have rubber tyres, which makes it quieter than most other systems. This method has been adopted in Montreal and Mexico City.

At present, railways carry more freight (goods) than passenger traffic. Many goods travel in standard-sized containers, which simplifies handling. There are tanker wagons for bulk liquids, multi-decked transporters for vehicles, and refrigerator vans for foodstuffs.

Metals

Man has been using metals for more than 5,000 years. In the modern world they form an essential part of everyday life. Steel is the main metal of all machinery, from motor-cars to giant presses. Copper cables carry electricity, water flows through pipes of iron, lead, or copper.

Metals make up a large part of the Earth's crust, but most of them are found combined with other substances. Many are in rocks, which are known as *ores*. Ores occur only in certain parts of the world, sometimes at great depths below the ground. In South Africa, for example, gold is mined 3.8 km (2.4 miles) below the surface.

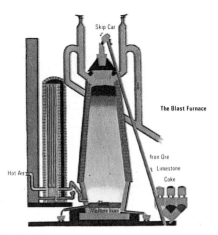

The Blast Furnace

The Blast Furnace

Smelting iron ore takes place in a *blast furnace*, so called because a blast of hot air passes through it.

Iron ore — a compound of iron and oxygen — is heated in the furnace with coke. The oxygen combines with the carbon in the coke to form a gas, which escapes. The iron remains behind. The hot-air blast through the furnace makes the coke burn fiercely. The temperature is high enough to melt the iron. Limestone is added to the furnace to help remove impurities. It combines with them to form a molten *slag*.

The blast furnace is a brick-lined cylinder as much as 30 metres (100 feet) high. Coke, iron ore, and limestone are fed into the top of the furnace. They are called the *charge*. The heat from the burning coke melts the iron, which runs down to the bottom of the furnace. The molten slag forms a layer on top of the iron.

Every few hours the molten iron is *tapped*, or drawn off. The iron produced in the furnace is called *pig iron*.

Left: Miners operate a powerful drilling tool to remove metal ores from deposits deep underground.

Many processes are needed to extract most metals from their ores. First of all unwanted material with the ore is removed, often simply by washing. But more complicated treatment may be needed, such as crushing or heating.

These processes leave a concentrated ore. Extracting the metal from this ore can be done in many ways, one of the most common being by heating the ore in a furnace. The metal when it is extracted may still contain other substances, called *impurities*. To obtain the pure metal, a process called *refining* follows.

There are various ways of shaping the metal once it is obtained. It can be *cast*, by melting it, pouring it into a mould and allowing it to cool. Hot metal can be pressed into shape by *forging*, or formed into sheets by *rolling*. Rods and tubes can be *extruded*—pushed into shape by forcing the metal through holes. Wires are made by *drawing* the cold metal through holes or between shaped rollers.

Right: A sheet of hot metal passes over rollers and under a water spray to cool it.

Below left: A large steel ingot is forged into shape under a powerful press.

Right: Automatic torches burning oxygen and propane cut out girders from thick sheet steel.

Below: Men pour molten metal into moulds to cast a large object.

Road Transport

People have made and used roads almost since the invention of the wheel about 5,000 years ago. The greatest of the ancient road-builders were the Romans, but after the Roman Empire roads they made in Europe fell into disrepair.

During the Industrial Revolution in the 18th century, people began to build good roads again. Fast stage coaches linked cities and crossed Europe and North America. The growth of railways in the 19th century ended the era of the stage coaches, and most roads carried only local traffic. Then in the 1880s the first motor-cars appeared, and roads began to come into their own again.

Today, all over the world railways are declining in importance and more goods are carried by road. Mass production, developed by Henry Ford in the United States in 1913, brought motor-cars within the reach of millions of people. Nowadays vast networks of highways have been constructed to link all the world's main cities.

Sedan Chair.

Eighteenth-century Phaeton.

Eighteenth-century mail coach.

Internal Combustion Engines

The internal combustion engine is so called because the fuel is burned inside the *cylinders* of the engine, instead of outside them to heat water and raise steam, as in the steam engine. The fuel used is either petrol or diesel oil.

In a petrol engine—the most usual for ordinary motor-cars and light goods vehicles—there are four or six cylinders. Inside each cylinder is a close-fitting *piston* which can slide up and down. The gases produced by burning the fuel push the piston down. The pistons are connected to a crankshaft and force it round, just as the pedals of a bicycle force the chainwheel round.

Most engines work on what is called a *four-stroke cycle*, in which power is produced in only one of each group of four movements of each piston. Smaller engines, such as those used for many motor-cycles, work on a two-stroke cycle, and produce power on every downward stroke.

The fuel is mixed with air in the *carburettor*, a device rather like a scent-spray, and sprayed into each cylinder

Above: Some early forms of road transport. The early 1800s were the heyday of the coach in Europe. In North America, stage-coaches flourished later until railways were built.

Right: A steam road carriage of the mid-19th century. The steam engine was to prove no rival to the petrol engine in the field of road transport.

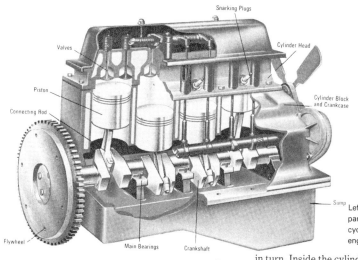

Left: The principal parts of a four-cyclinder petrol engine.

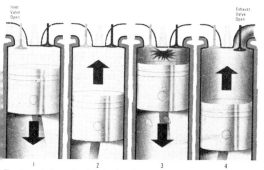

The four-stroke cycle. 1, Induction Stroke. The piston moves down the cylinder, drawing down a mixture of petrol and air into the cylinder. 2, Compression Stroke. The piston moves up, compressing the petrol and air mixture. 3, Power Stroke. The petrol-and-air mixture is ignited by an electric spark. The rapid expansion of the hot gases drives the piston downwards. 4, Exhaust Stroke. The piston moves upwards and the spent gases are forced out of the cylinder.

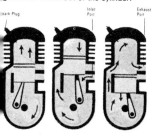

Left: The two-stroke cycle, where power is produced on every downward stroke. 1, Upward compression stroke. 2, Downward power stroke. 3, Lower part of downward stroke where spent gases are expelled and fresh fuel enters the cylinder.

in turn. Inside the cylinder, it is ignited by a spark, produced when a current of electricity jumps across between the metal points of a *sparking plug*. A rotating arm in the *distributor* feeds the electricity to each sparking plug in turn.

The electricity comes from a *battery*, which is charged continually by a *dynamo* or an *alternator* driven by the engine. The battery also provides power for lights, windscreen wipers and other accessories.

Other Kinds of Engines

Diesel engines, used in most heavy trucks, differ from petrol engines because they have no sparking plugs or carburettors. Diesel oil is injected directly into each cylinder, and is burned by heat produced when air is compressed in the cylinders.

Vehicles which do not have to travel long distances or at high speeds are sometimes driven by electric motors, powered by batteries. The batteries have to be recharged every night. Research has been underway for some time to produce more efficient batteries which give higher speeds and longer distances.

Ships and the Sea

People have been going to sea in ships for at least 6,000 years. The earliest ships we know about were slender vessels, driven by many oars, which the Egyptians used to sail to Crete. Such a ship had a single square sail to help if the wind was in the right direction. Today, more than 70,000 ships cross the world's oceans. They include giant tankers more than 400 metres (1,300 feet) long.

The Age of Sail

The combination of oars and sail continued up to about A.D. 100. Then a new kind of sail was developed, called a *lateen* sail. It was triangular, and it enabled ships to sail close to the wind—that is, almost against it—as well as with the wind. By about 1400 sailors had developed the *full-rigged ship*, which had a foremast and mainmast with square sails and at the stern a mizzenmast with a lateen sail. Over the centuries the number of sails on each mast increased, and in the largest and latest sailing ships was six or more.

Ancient Egyptian trading vessel.

Viking longship.

Medieval ship with lateen sails.

Early steamship.

The age of sail lasted until the late 1800s, and overlapped with the advent of steamships. Sailing ships are still used for pleasure and adventure.

The Age of Steam

The first steamships were built in the late 1700s. By the mid-1800s powered ships burning wood and coal were rapidly replacing sailing ships. At first, steamships were driven by paddle-wheels at the sides. Then the screw propeller was invented, and proved to be far superior. It has remained in use to this day. Also during the 1800s, first iron and then steel replaced wood as the main material from which ships were built.

In the 1890s, Charles Parsons, an English engineer, developed the steam turbine as an engine for driving ships. Within a few years every fast ship had turbines. From the 1920s onwards, oil largely replaced coal as the main fuel. Today, most steamships use oil. Some ships are driven by diesel engines, which work on the same principle as those used to power trucks. A few ships are powered by nuclear energy, but it has so far proved too expensive to use, except in submarines.

Top left: The first commercially successful steamboat, the *Clermont*, was built in 1807 by the American engineer Robert Fulton.

Bottom left: The *Savannah* was the first ship to use steam during an Atlantic crossing. Her voyage took 29 days.

Below: The *Cutty Sark*, one of the great sailing ships.

Right: The launching of an American nuclear-powered submarine. Ships are built close to water on a slipway, down which they slide when they are launched.

1   2   3   4   5

Above: Stages in ship-building: 1. First stage with plating complete; 2. Main watertight bulkheads erected; 3. Completing plating and bulkheads for F deck; 4. Deckhouse bulkheads in position on E deck; 5. B and C decks and the stern take shape.

Navigation

Sailors use several methods to *navigate* or find their way across the featureless oceans. The most important instrument is the *compass*, which always points towards the north. The simplest form of compass is magnetic, but most large ships today use a *gyrocompass*, which contains a rapidly spinning gyroscope wheel. Such a device also points to the north.

Navigators also use *chronometers*, which give them a very accurate time. They frequently check their position by observing the position of heavenly bodies in the sky—the Sun by day and the stars and planets by night. A navigator measures the angle of sev-

eral stars against the horizon, and with the aid of tables he can find out where he should be, given the time of day. In *dead reckoning*, the navigator plots on a chart the distance his ship has travelled and the direction. He uses a *log* to tell him how far he has travelled.

Modern methods of navigation include *radio direction finders*, which can tell from which direction a known radio signal—such as from a radio beacon on a lighthouse—has come. By getting a 'fix' on two radio signals, the navigator can calculate his position.

Navigators use *radar* to detect objects close to the ship, such as other shipping or a coastline. The radar 'bounces' signals off the objects.

The Story of Flight

In 1903, two American brothers, Wilbur and Orville Wright, built a flimsy flying machine which was powered by a petrol engine. On December 17, Orville made the first-ever powered flight on a deserted stretch of sand at Kitty Hawk, in North Carolina. That flight lasted only 36 metres (120 feet) but it marked the start of the age of the aeroplane.

Airships and Balloons

Man had been trying to fly for hundreds of years before the Wright Brothers' triumph, but his earlier successes had been with craft that were lighter than air—balloons and airships. The first balloons were filled with hot air, which rises because it is lighter than the cold air surrounding it.

More efficient balloons were made to be filled with *hydrogen*, a gas which is 14 times lighter than air. Its main disadvantage is that it burns very readily. Most gas-filled balloons today contain *helium*, which is heavier than hydrogen, but does not burn.

Balloons can go only where the wind

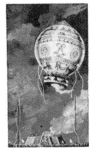

Above: The first manned balloon flight was made in France on October 15, 1783, in a hot-air balloon designed and made by brothers Joseph and Etienne Montgolfier.

Below: The airship *Hindenberg*, one of the last Zeppelins to be built. On May 6, 1937, the *Hindenberg* exploded at Lakehurst, New Jersey, with the loss of 36 lives. This was the last of a series of disasters which led to the end of airships.

blows them. In the late 1800s men built cigar-shaped balloons which were driven by steam engines and were *dirigible*—that is, they could be steered. In 1900, Count Ferdinand von Zeppelin, a German engineer, built the first really successful *airship*, powered by the recently developed petrol engine. Airships successfully carried passengers and mail for some years, but a series of disasters in the 1930s led all countries to abandon airships in favour of aeroplanes.

Piston Engines and Jets

Aeroplanes—heavier-than-air craft—can fly because of the shape of their wings. These have what is called an *aerofoil* cross-section. When the plane moves forwards, the flow of air over the wings produces *lift*.

The first aeroplanes were powered by piston engines, working on the same principle as those of motor-cars (see pages 112–113), and driving a *propeller*, which screws its way through the air. Jet engines, developed in the 1940s, are now used for all very large and fast aircraft. A jet engine burns fuel inside it and gives off hot gases, which *exhaust* through an aperture at

the rear. The reaction inside the engine to this exhaust provides the thrust which drives the engine, and propels the aircraft.

The fuel used in jet engines is kerosene (paraffin), which is much cheaper than petrol and a lot safer to handle. They use huge quantities: for a flight across the Atlantic Ocean a jet airliner has to carry more than 90,000 litres (20,000 gallons) of fuel.

Helicopters

Most aeroplanes can fly only straight forward, though some, such as the Harrier jump-jet military aircraft, can take off and land vertically by directing the thrust of their jets downwards. But the most versatile flying machine is the helicopter, which can not only go straight up and down, but can also hover like a fly and go forwards, backwards, and sideways. It does not need a long prepared runway on which to get up speed. It can operate from a flat roof in a city or from a jungle clearing with equal ease.

Helicopters have a top speed of only about 320 kph (200 mph), which is nowhere near as fast as normal fixed-wing aeroplanes. But their manoeuvre-

Above: The wing of a plane is sharply curved at the top and fairly flat at the bottom. Air passing over the top surface travels faster than the air passing beneath because it has further to go. This means that the air pressure above the wing is less than that below it. The suction produced in this way provides the 'lift' necessary to keep a plane in the air.

ability has made them invaluable for inter-city transport, sea rescue, spraying crops, fighting forest fires, moving troops, lifting heavy loads, and hundreds of other uses.

The helicopter has often been called the 'flying windmill' because of the *rotor*—a set of three rotating blades—on the top of its body. This main rotor serves as both the propeller and the wings, providing both lift and thrust. The rotor blades have the same aerofoil shape as wings and ordinary propeller blades.

When the main rotor turns, the body of the helicopter tends to spin in the opposite direction. To counteract this movement, a small rotor is mounted vertically on the tail. The sideways thrust produced by this tail rotor just balances the turning tendency of the helicopter body. Both rotors are driven by the same engine. Some very large helicopters have two main rotors, turning in opposite directions so that their twisting motions cancel out.

Movement of the helicopter in any direction is achieved simply by varying the *pitch* of the rotor blades. Pitch is the angle at which the blades slice through the air.

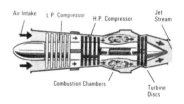

Above: In a jet engine, compressed air from a compressor is fed into the combustion chambers with a jet of fuel and the mixture is ignited. Before the hot gases escape from the jet pipe at the rear, they turn a turbine which drives the compressor.

Left: Practical knowledge gained from early glider flights helped to pave the way for powered aircraft.

Food and Farming

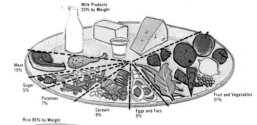

Farming is the world's greatest and most important industry. Without farming, there would be no food for the world's rapidly increasing population —4,400 million in the early 1980s.

Farmers grow many kinds of crops, both as food and to provide raw materials such as fibres and rubber. The most important food crops are *cereals*, such as wheat, rice, and maize (corn in the U.S.A.). Wheat is the leading bread grain and is one of the most widely grown crops. Rice is even more important because it forms the staple diet of about half of the world's people. Nine-tenths of the world's rice is grown and eaten in Asia. *Potatoes* rival cereals as a source of food. They yield more per area than any cereals.

During the present century, mechanization has brought great changes to farming. The number of people working on the land has decreased, but each worker produces much more food. The main item of farm machinery is the tractor, which is used to pull many kinds of implements over the land. These implements include *ploughs* to turn the soil over, *cultivators* to break it up, *sprayers* to spray

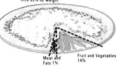

Above: A typical daily diet in the U.S.A. compared with the daily diet of an Indian worker. The weight of food eaten by an American is nearly three times that eaten by the Indian, and the protein content is far greater.

Right: The combine harvester has done much to increase the world's food output. It has made possible the great wheat fields of North America which sometimes stretch unbroken to the horizon.

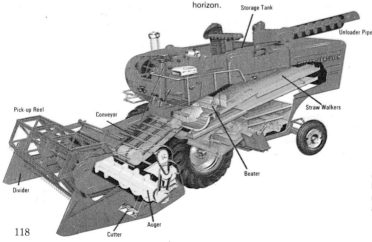

Left: Simplified diagram of a combine harvester, one of the most valuable agricultural machines.

insecticides on to the growing crops and kill pests which would eat the food, *mowing machines* and *balers* for hay. Specialized machines harvest crops. The biggest are the *combine harvesters* which gather wheat and similar crops. The machines cut the wheat, thresh it to extract the edible seeds, and drop the cut stalks back on the ground. Other machines are used for picking crops such as cotton or fruit.

Farm machinery is also used to help raise livestock. Many cows are milked by electric milking machines, and other animals are fed by conveyors.

Subsistence Farming

Although the developed countries of the world use a great many machines on their farms, large numbers of people still cultivate the soil by primitive means. Many of them can grow only enough food for their families. This is *subsistence* farming.

Work is going on under the United Nations to help such people farm more efficiently, and to provide them with seeds that will give them bigger crops.

Above: Ploughing the rice paddies with buffaloes in South East Asia.

Left: Plantation crops such as tea are grown commercially in tropical lands but are mainly for export.

Below: The intensive rearing of animals has played a large part in meeting the growing food demands in the West.

119

Computers

In the past quarter-century computers have come to play a major part in people's everyday lives. For example, a man may receive wages that are worked out by a computer, bills made out by computer, and advertising mail addressed by a computer. He reads books that are type-set by computer, and if he works in a factory many of the machines there may well be controlled by computers. He sees on TV how astronauts travel in space—and every detail of their flights, even to the Moon, is controlled by batteries of computers.

Kinds of Computers

Basically, a computer is a calculating machine, which can work out problems many millions of times faster than the human brain. It can also store information, and produce any part of it when asked to do so. Computers range in size from vast machines which occupy a whole room to small ones which can be held in the hand. Even the popular pocket calculator is a simple form of computer, which can perform limited functions only. Some computers can perform a range of tasks; others are built to do one job only, such as control a machine tool.

There are two main kinds of computers: *digital* computers and *analogue* computers. Digital computers are the most common. They deal in separate numbers, as does an abacus (a bead frame for counting) or a cash register. They are used in accounting, banking, and performing all sorts of high-speed mathematical calculations.

A digital computer 'counts' using the *binary* system of numbers. Instead of counting in 10s, as we do normally, it counts in 2s. The binary system uses only two numbers, 0 and 1. The figure one is represented by 1, just as in the *decimal* system (counting in 10s). Two is 10, three is 11, four is 100, and so on. In computer language, these binary digits are called *bits*. They are very easy for an electrical circuit to handle: 1 is represented by the current being on, and 0 by it being off. The thousands of minute electronic circuits inside a computer can switch on and off so fast that the computer can perform calculations almost at once.

An analogue computer works with continuously varying information, which is represented by physical quantities which it can handle. A very simple form is the slide rule, in which a number is represented by a marked off strip of plastic. In electronic analogue computers, quantities are represented by electric voltages, which may vary continuously. They are used, for example, in *simulators* for training the pilots of aircraft. When the pilot moves the controls in the flightdeck of a simulator, varying electric signals pass to the analogue computer, which works out what would happen to a real aircraft.

A pocket calculator is a device which performs calculations, but cannot process the many kinds of information that a computer does.

Above: Compact computer systems like this can be used by small businesses.

Diagnosis by computer is now used by many doctors, in this case to diagnose a tumour.

Using Computers

A digital computer has five main parts, no matter how big or small it is. First comes the *input unit*, through which information is fed to the computer. This is usually a keyboard, rather like that of a typewriter. A *visual display* (a screen like a TV set) shows the operator what is being fed into the machine—just as a typist can see on paper the words that are typed.

The *main memory* stores information that is fed into the computer, and also holds the *instructions* with which the computer has been *programmed*. A programme tells the computer to perform certain tasks in a particular order. These instructions are selected by the machine's *control unit*. Under these instructions, the *arithmetic/logic unit* carries out all the calculations required.

Finally, the *output unit* translates all the results of the calculations and shows them up in a form that can be readily understood, either on a visual display or as a *print-out* on paper. It can also ask the operator questions or to perform certain functions and feed in more information via the input unit.

The abacus is one of the oldest calculating devices known. It was known to the ancient Babylonians and Chinese.

A Brunsviga mechanical calculator made in 1892.

Below: A major computer set-up of today. The use of transistors and micro-chips has enabled powerful computers to be condensed into a small space.

Civil Engineering

The world's biggest and most spectacular structures include dams, bridges, waterways, highroads, tunnels, and airports. The design and construction of such structures form an important branch of engineering called *civil engineering.*

Bridges and Roads

The simplest kind of bridge consists of a long *beam*, or piece of timber or steel, supported at the ends by *piers*. But the span—the distance between supports —of a beam bridge cannot be too great or the bridge will collapse under its own weight.

For greater spans, an *arch bridge* can be used. With an arch the weight of the bridge is transmitted at an angle down both sides to supporting *abutments*. Arch bridges are very strong. Some built by the Romans more than 2,000 years ago are still standing. They were built of stone or brick. Modern arch bridges are often built of steel. The longest steel arch bridge is Sydney Harbour Bridge in Australia, which has a span of 502 metres (1,650 feet).

Above: Spinning the wire cables of the suspension bridge over the River Forth, in Scotland. The bridge was completed in 1964. In the background is the Forth rail bridge, a cantilever bridge built in 1890.

Right: This spectacular viaduct carries a railway across a steep valley in Switzerland. The shape of the arches gives the bridge its strength. The load is carried down the arches to the supporting piers and to the sides of the valley.

Left: The busy Los Angeles Freeway. Multi-lane highways are needed to cope with the ever increasing volume of traffic. Today, there are well over 200 million road vehicles in the world—nearly half of them in the U.S.A.

In a *suspension bridge*, the roadway hangs from a pair of cables carried by two towers, one on either bank. The cables are made of thousands of strong steel wires, and the deck hangs from them by steel rods, called *suspenders.*

A *cantilever bridge* is a form of beam bridge in which the beam is supported by a pier at its middle. One end of the beam is anchored to the bank. The other end reaches out to meet a similar cantilevered beam from the opposite bank.

Bridges carry roads and railways. The first step in constructing a road is to survey the ground, and to bore holes to find out what kind of soil or rock lies underneath. If the soil is loose, it must be strengthened by mixing gravel or sand with it, or by rolling or ramming it to make it firm.

The road is built with the aid of earth-moving machinery, such as excavators and bulldozers. To make it as level as possible, some parts must be built up and others cut away. The road is then surfaced, either with a rigid layer of concrete, or with a flexible layer of broken stones, held together by tar. It is called *tarmacadam*.

Tunnels and Dams

It is often necessary when building roads or railways to drive tunnels through hills and under mountains in order to avoid a steep, winding route. In hard rock, tunnels are driven by blasting with explosives. In soft ground, a *tunnelling shield* is used to

Below: A combined excavator and tunnel shield. The tunnel shield was invented by the British engineer Marc Brunel for boring tunnels through clay or soft rock. In the 140 years since the shield was invented, many modifications have been made but the principles remain the same. Under the protection of the shield the clay is dug out. As the *spoil* is removed the shield is jacked forward.

support the soil while it is dug away and a steel and concrete lining is built.

Dams are used to hold back water and create huge artificial lakes called reservoirs. These reservoirs store water to supply cities. The biggest dams are giant mounds of earth and rock packed tightly together. An *earthen* dam of this kind has a very wide base and gradually tapers towards the top. It is usually faced with steel and concrete to make it watertight.

Other dams are built of concrete or stone blocks. *Arch dams* are used in narrow gorges. They are curved towards the water in the shape of an arch, which makes them very strong.

Other activities of civil engineering include the construction of large buildings such as skyscrapers.

Man in Space

Astronautics is the branch of science which deals with the many problems of space flight. The Space Age began with the launching of the artificial satellite *Sputnik 1* on October 4, 1957. Already, Man has reached the Moon and unmanned *probes* have been sent to Jupiter, Saturn and other parts of the Solar System.

After months of training, the astronauts—known as cosmonauts in Russia—climb into their spacecraft and are blasted into space on top of a massive rocket. The rocket gives the spacecraft the high speed needed to escape from the Earth's gravitational pull.

Out in space the effect of gravity is much less, and the astronauts, like everything else, are weightless. Nothing keeps them 'down' and they can float around freely. Eating and drinking are very different from on Earth. Food and drink must be squeezed right into the mouth.

The crew cabin of the spacecraft is connected to what is known as a *life-support system*. This provides gas

Above: A Vostok spacecraft on top of its launching rocket.

Above: The Skylab 4/Saturn 1B is launched from Kennedy Space Centre on November 16, 1973.

Left: An astronaut 'walks' in space tethered to his spacecraft.

under pressure for the astronauts to breathe, removes stale air and moisture, and keeps the temperature steady.

Returning to Earth is one of the most dangerous aspects of space flight. If an ordinary spacecraft is in orbit round the Earth, *retro-rockets* are fired to slow it down and gravity draws it towards the ground. The capsule containing the astronauts then separates from the rest of the craft. As the capsule re-enters the atmosphere the air acts like a brake, slowing it down and heating it at the same time. The base of the capsule glows red-hot, but it is specially designed as a *heat-shield* to protect the astronauts. As the capsule falls lower, parachutes open and gently carry it down to the ground or the sea.

Re-entry after a round trip to the Moon is even more difficult. The capsule is travelling at almost 40,000 kph (25,000 mph), and it must enter the atmosphere at a precise point. With the Space Shuttle, the complete spacecraft returns to Earth and can make several flights.

Rockets

Rockets burn fuel to produce a jet of hot gases which shoot out backwards and drive the vehicle forwards. Rockets can operate in the vacuum of space because they carry their own oxygen as well as fuel. The substance that provides oxygen to burn the fuel is called an *oxidant*. Both fuel and oxidant are called *propellants*.

A single rocket cannot by itself launch a heavy load into space. A number of rockets must be linked in stages, one on top of the other to provide enough power. Most space vehicles have a massive first stage, or *booster*, and two smaller stages. Each stage fires in turn and thrusts the vehicle higher and higher. The vehicle gets lighter and lighter as each spent stage falls away.

Right: The Space Shuttle Columbia on its second launch on November 12, 1981.

American astronauts first set foot on the Moon on July 21, 1969.

Steps in Space

1957 The Soviet Union launched *Sputnik 1*, the first artificial satellite.

1958 The U.S.A. launched its first satellite, *Explorer 1*, in January.

1959 Space probes reached the Moon and took pictures of its far side.

1961 Yuri Gagarin (Soviet Union) in *Vostok 1* became the first man in space on April 12, making one orbit of the Earth.

1962 John Glenn in *Friendship 7* became the first American in space.

1963 Valentina Tereshkova (Soviet Union) became the first woman cosmonaut.

1965 Alexei Leonov (Soviet Union) made the first 'walk' in space.

1966 *Luna 9* (Soviet Union) made the first true soft Moon landing.

Gemini 8 (U.S.) made the first successful docking, or link-up manoeuvre, with another vehicle in space.

1968 Frank Borman, James Lovell and William Anders in *Apollo 8* became the first men to travel to the Moon and back.

1969 *Apollo 11* landed the first man on the Moon. On July 21 Neil Armstrong stepped from the lunar module on to the Moon's surface. On November 19, American astronauts again landed on the Moon.

1970 In April, an explosion in *Apollo 13* almost brought disaster to the mission.

1971 *Apollo 14* (February) and *Apollo 15* (August) continued Moon exploration.

1972 *Apollo 16* (April) and *Apollo 17*

(December) completed the Moon programme.

1973 In May, U.S. launched Space Station *Skylab* into a near-Earth orbit.

1974 U.S. probe *Mariner 10* passed Venus and Mercury for close-up looks.

1975 U.S. and Soviet Union combined with the Apollo-Soyuz link-up in space.

1976 Space probes landed on Mars, found no sign of life.

1980 U.S. space probes discovered new moons and rings around Jupiter. Soviet cosmonauts spent a record 175 days in space. Skylab fell to Earth.

1981 U.S. space shuttle made its first flight. Space probes photographed Saturn.

Cover photographs: Kay Muldoon/Colorific,
Andy Williams Photo Library, Malcolm Aird Associates,
Robin Kerrod

Acknowledgements
We gratefully acknowlege the assistance of the following
organizations in assembling photographic material for
this encyclopaedia:
Air India, Bryan and Cherry Alexander, Anglo-American
Corporation of South Africa Limited, Arab Information
Centre, Sir William Arrol & Company Limited, Australian
News & Information Bureau, Biofotos, Bowaters U.K.
Paper Company Limited, The British Petroleum
Company Limited, Canadian Film Board, Canadian
Government Travel Bureau, Central Office of
Information, Ceylon Tea Centre, Consolidated Gold
Fields Limited, Thomas Cook & Son Limited, Courtaulds
Limited, French Government Tourist Office, French Line,
German Embassy, Granada Television, Greek Tourist
Office, Hewlett Packard, Houston Chamber of
Commerce, I.C.I. Plastics Division, Imperial Government
of Iran, Infoplan Limited, Israel Government Tourist
Office, Italian State Tourist Office, Japan Airlines
Company Limited, Japanese Embassy, The Mansell
Collection, Middle East Airlines, A. Monk and Company
Limited, Moroccan Embassy, NASA, National Portrait
Gallery, New Zealand High Commission, Novosti Press
Agency, Pan American Airways, Peruvian Embassy,
Paul Popper Photo, Port of London Authority, The
Science Museum, Shell Chemicals United Kingdom
Limited, South African Airways, Sun Alliance and
London Insurance Group, Trans Antarctic Expedition,
Uganda High Commission, Union Castle Line, United
States Embassy, United States Naval Forces in Europe,
Walker Art Gallery, Liverpool, Zambian National Tourist
Bureau.